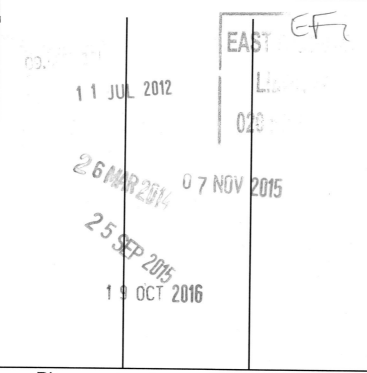

the best way to create sacred space, the elements required for
an altar, or some inspiration to deepen your meditation
practice, it's at your fingertips in this book.

CONNIE KAPLAN, Doctor of Ministry, author of *The Woman's Book
of Dreams, Dreams Are Letters from the Soul,* and *The Invisible Garment*

In an age when many conventional religious paths have lost their meaning, each person must find their own relationship to the spiritual journey often outside established structures. Lara Owen does a masterful job of offering a rich and practical variety of avenues to explore one's own spiritual path.

TSULTRIM ALLIONE, author of *Women of Wisdom* and *Feeding Your Demons*

∞∞

*Growing Your Inner Light* is a beautifully written and inspiring spiritual guide for those of an independent heart and mind. You will find it full of helpful jewels and practical wisdom, whether you are experienced or new to spirituality, and whatever your tradition or belief system.

WILLIAM BLOOM, PHD, author of *Soulution* and *The Endorphin Effect* and founder of the Foundation for Holistic Spirituality

∞∞

*Growing Your Inner Light* will help you develop presence and awareness. Lara Owen captures a beautiful simplicity while weaving together the vital threads that compose a doable daily spiritual practice. She gives us a menu of options for ways to realign with our soul and source, and writes cleanly, without the clutter of unnecessary words. The overall effect is an experience of sweetness and peace, which is always the marker of true Spirit.

PENNEY PEIRCE, intuition expert and author of *Frequency* and *The Intuitive Way*

# GROWING
## YOUR INNER
# LIGHT

# LARA OWEN

# GROWING YOUR INNER LIGHT

## A GUIDE TO INDEPENDENT SPIRITUAL PRACTICE

piatkus

PIATKUS

First published in the US in 2009 by Atria Paperback/Beyond Words,
a division of Simon & Schuster, Inc.
First published in Great Britain in 2011 by Piatkus

A CIP catalogue record for this book
is available from the British Library.

ISBN 978-0-7499-5408-6

Printed and bound in Great Britain by
Clays Ltd, St Ives plc

Papers used by Piatkus are natural, renewable and
recyclable products sourced from well-managed forests and certified
in accordance with the rules of the Forest Stewardship Council.

Mixed Sources
Product group from well-managed
forests and other controlled sources
www.fsc.org Cert no. SGS-COC-004081
© 1996 Forest Stewardship Council
FSC

Piatkus
An imprint of
Little, Brown Book Group
100 Victoria Embankment
London EC4Y 0DY

An Hachette UK Company
www.hachette.co.uk

www.piatkus.co.uk

*To all my teachers*

# CONTENTS

# PREFACE

● ◐ ○ ○ ○ ◐ ◑ ●

Our sense of Spirit is embedded deep within us. Something we cannot see, dissect, or measure impels us to perform acts of worship, to better ourselves, to overcome tragedy, to create works of art that inspire and uplift, to love others even when they have done us harm, to rescue those in need, and to seek inner peace. This Spirit lives both within us and independently of us, permeating everything: land and flora, birds and animals, oceans and skies.

Each culture describes Spirit in its own way: Tibetan Buddhists see many celestial beings, including sky goddesses called *dakinis* who help liberate us from our clinging to ego; the monotheistic faiths — Christianity, Islam, Judaism — see a male God who overlooks our human world, loves us, and intervenes at crucial times; Native Americans see a world in which the Great Spirit imbues nature and teaches us through the wisdom of living creatures, the weather, and our fundamental connection to the Earth; Amazonian tribes see Spirit in vegetation, ritually ingesting plants such as *ayahuasca* in order to connect with special kinds of wisdom; and Hindu yogis purify the body through exercises designed to open the inner channels. There are many ways to meet the energies we often call God, and which in this book I call Spirit.

Finding our own path to Spirit in this multicultural, rapidly changing twenty-first century world takes some application. For many people today, organized religion does not appeal (for varying reasons), so there is often no local, easily integrated, traditional way forward. The quest to connect has become a journey with many potential paths, some of which lead to dead ends and are merely quick fixes rooted in "me first" materialism. But the attempt must be made, and we have many time-honored methods for honoring the ineffable wonder residing inside ourselves and in the outer world. The urge to develop the inner spirit and connect with the outer spirit is irrepressible; it is hard-wired into human nature.

I dedicate this book to that timeless human longing for the sublime, that undying urge to explore and offer up the very best we can be, the most we can do, the heart of our humanity.

# Introduction

# THE INDEPENDENT PATH

● ◗ ◖ ○ ◐ ◗ ●

There is a time-honored tradition of independent spiritual practice. After all, Jesus and the Buddha were both independent spiritual practitioners, and many saints and holy men and women have found their deepest sense of Spirit through a very private communion, whether outside, within, or in conflict with organized religion. Over the past few decades, more and more people have found themselves disillusioned by traditional religious institutions yet still wanting an active spiritual connection. They have chosen to follow an independent journey, traveling the path without the comfort and support, nor the limitation or restriction, of an organized sect or religion.

I've been on a conscious quest to have an authentic relationship with Spirit since I was fourteen years old. The church of my childhood—the Church of England—had been a big influence on me and a source of much comfort and enjoyment until adolescence began. At that time, I started to think more deeply and found I had many questions that the Church seemed unable to answer. One Sunday, while listening to a sermon on the evils of fornication given by an overzealous curate, I had an epiphany, a radical shift in my awareness.

Despite my youth and relative innocence, I realized I could not follow a religion that in any way made the body, particularly sexuality, a sin. In a flash of understanding, I saw that my life force was suppressed in the Church in a way that I could not, and should not, tolerate.

I did throw the baby out with the bathwater, it's true, but there was simply not enough juice to hold me in the Church. Along with many of my rock-and-roll generation, I was already aware of my affinity with dance, rhythmic music, and nature, and I had a growing interest in ecstatic states of body and mind. All this felt holy to me, and in the 1970s my local church was the antithesis of this developing sense of spirituality. I found that I experienced awe and connection by being in nature and other physically rooted experiences, and in these contexts I felt spiritually nourished. So it's no surprise that, like many of my peers, the spiritual paths with which I later found significant resonance were Taoism, Buddhism, and the indigenous traditions of the Americas and the British Isles.

Over the past thirty years, I've studied many spiritual traditions and incorporated whatever worked into a mélange of influences that to some might seem dizzying. For me, and for many people I know who have created their own version of a spiritual life, this freedom to integrate from different traditions—and to make up new ones—feels rich and nourishing. But like any path worth taking, a syncretic and creative approach is not without potential difficulties. By anchoring ourselves within practices that are found cross-culturally, and by maintaining good contact with our native common sense, we can avoid getting lost or running aground. The thirteen lessons in this book are designed to assist in this process.

Let me make it clear that, in discussing independent spiritual practice, I am not advocating that you avoid contact with spiritual teachers or traditions. On the contrary, I think that such exposure is invaluable for anyone seriously interested in their spiritual development. It's not an either-or. You can go to a church, temple, or mosque, study with spiritual teachers, and attend whichever religious gatherings attract you. The distinction is that you are in charge of your own spiritual journey. As an independent spiritual practitioner, you don't have a specific identity: you're not only a Buddhist or a Catholic or a pagan or a follower of Sai Baba or Sai Anybody. This does not mean that you are a dilettante who is not serious about your spiritual life. It's possible for you to go very deep as an independent practitioner, because your journey stays authentic.

By maintaining your center of gravity within your own experience, perception and ability to discriminate, you are far less likely to be steered astray or limited in your spiritual development by a charismatic leader or an inflexible tradition. The only dangers you have to deal with are those generated by your own failings, and by approaching them head-on rather than projecting them onto a teacher, you stand a chance of going a long, long way in your spiritual development.

My task in writing this book has been to simplify and clarify, wherever possible, the practices I have found most useful. I am aware of the contemporary trap of diluting ancient wisdom so that it becomes anodyne and ineffective, and I have worked hard to avoid this. Despite being extracted from their traditions and married with those from other places, the practices I discuss and describe here are still potent, and will be activated and individualized by the application of your own consciousness and intention. I have looked for practices that occur across all or many of the traditions, and this has been particularly straightforward and obvious when drawing from the more earth-centered ways of entering into communion with the divine.

## DEVELOPING INNER PEACE

Ultimately, we probably don't need any practices at all in order to develop spiritually. Spiritual development throughout the course of one's life is a natural part of being human, nourished by loving relationships and by moments that engender awe and a sense of connection to everything. People who live good lives naturally grow in compassion and wisdom. As they age, they radiate an inner peace.

The two great keys to this development occurring relatively unhindered are humility and authenticity (the ability to be real, transparent, and honest in relationship with yourself and with others). Humility has always been encouraged by religion but authenticity rather less so, due to the inevitable consequence of organization of belief by rules and laws. However, many religious leaders do support the flowering of genuine expression and the development of a whole and authentic personality.

Even though spiritual development is a natural process, modern life, with its materialist focus, intense level of stimulation, and tendency to separate us from the natural world, makes spiritual maturity something most of us need to consciously engage with to move toward. If we decide to do this, the technology of spiritual practice developed throughout history by people all over the world is a resource that can make our progress smoother. This is part of our humanity: spiritually oriented actions such as prayers and rituals occur cross-culturally and seem to be innate in human nature.

Just as we exercise our bodies, we can also exercise our spiritual muscles. We can choose to consciously develop our spiritual sensibility. We live in complicated times, and developing inner strength is just as important as developing physical health and well-being. This inner work helps us make life choices that are in harmony with our inner being — choices that give us the chance to develop in spiritual depth and genuine wisdom throughout our lives.

## ORGANIZED RELIGION AND HERESY

Sometimes people express concern that if they don't belong to a specific religion and stay loyal only to that belief system, they will run adrift or, even worse, offend some spiritual authority, with dire consequences. Such beliefs are ancient, coming down to us through family and social history in our memories of pogroms and expulsions, which were based on issues of faith and rooted in the atavistic fear of being cast out of the tribe. The burning of witches in Europe in the

Middle Ages created a legacy of fear about independent spirituality, particularly about female spiritual authority and autonomy, just as it was designed to do. To be branded a rebel and heretic was punishable by death, and thus the word *heretic* came to have dark and clouded associations.

From a conventional perspective, by not belonging to one order and not buying into the whole package of one religion, everyone who undertakes an independent spiritual path might be considered a heretic.

Yet *heretic* originally meant something rather different. The word comes to us from the Greek *hairetikos*, meaning "able to choose." To be a heretic was simply being someone who chose for themselves.

## THE QUEST FOR ENLIGHTENMENT

Sometimes people are drawn into spiritual practice because they have heard of enlightenment and they imagine it means the end of all their pain and suffering. I have found it more useful to think of the spiritual journey as a gradually growing intensity of inner light throughout life, rather than as a sudden blast. This is much more practical, and it doesn't stress the body and mind with too much spiritual ambition.

This book aims to help you develop ways of gradually coming into greater inner peace, of slowly turning up the light inside you, with gentleness and kindness. It's not dramatic, it's not glamorous, it's not spiritual showbiz, but with steady application over time, it works.

## ADVANTAGES OF PURSUING AN INDEPENDENT SPIRITUAL PATH

Perhaps the most obvious advantage in this era of cults, sects, and abuse scandals is that by keeping yourself independent, you won't fall in with a coercive cult or a leader who is manipulative or corrupt. But that's like saying if you don't have a romantic relationship with anyone, you won't have your heart broken, which is a weak excuse for not living fully. So as a reason for pursuing an independent spiritual path, it really won't do. There are better ones.

By taking responsibility for your own spiritual development, you can follow your own sense of what is right for you. For example, if you have a period in which nature is your primary teacher and you feel drawn to spend time alone in the wild, you can do that. If life brings you a series of synchronicities about a certain teacher or discipline and you feel attracted to that work, you are free to follow that path for as long as you want. If you go through a stage where your attention is strongly focused on making a living or building a new relationship, then that becomes your spiritual work. Your spiritual path is completely intertwined with your life; it's not something you do only on Sundays or for a half hour in the morning.

You're not limited to any one doctrine, school, or creed. You can eat at whichever spiritual restaurant you like and pick from the menu according to your current needs. You can sit at the feet of the Dalai Lama for a four-day teaching, go on a ten-day Vipassana retreat, go to midnight Mass on Christmas Eve, go to a Druid solstice ritual, or find spiritual sustenance in all these places.

You can follow your own timing in your practice. If you feel overwhelmed by a series of intense experiences, you can back off and simply "chop wood, carry water"[1] for a while. If you begin to feel out of touch with yourself, you can create a retreat by using the tools that work best for you and by drawing from the techniques outlined here.

Your own path can be as simple or as elaborate as you like. While most things in life seem to work better the simpler and less encumbered we can keep them, the level of complexity of your explorations of spirituality, either in terms of how you think about it or how you actually do it, is very much a matter of individual preference.

In terms of ideology and the intellectual level of spirituality, some people love to have long conversations about what something actu-

---

1. "Chop wood, carry water" is an old Zen expression that refers to the practical necessity and spiritual value of simply getting on with ordinary life.

ally means and to define terms. They feel more grounded once they have an idea clearly stated. Others have an instinctual relationship with Spirit and feel no need for intellectual clarification. In general, it's a good idea to strike a balance here and not get too heady about spirituality, nor foster ungrounded beliefs that overwhelm your common sense.

In terms of rituals and styles of practice, this is, again, very much an individual matter, and I explore this more fully in the following chapters. What I want to stress here is that your spiritual practice may be very simple but nonetheless effective. Simplicity and clarity are advantages of the independent path. Religious organizations have to work for a lot of people and inevitably get caught up in politics, often becoming ideologically and ritualistically complex, far more so than is actually necessary for spiritual development.

You may already have a simple, spiritually nourishing daily practice without recognizing it as such. For example, going out to the garden first thing and admiring the flowers and trees is a form of practice that gives you a nature-based, reflective start to the day. But there are times when an elaborate ritual or practice is absolutely what is required to allow for an enhanced level of perception and a deeper level of integration than simple practice can supply.

## COMMON PITFALLS IN SPIRITUAL QUEST

There are several common pitfalls in the spiritual quest, and we are all prone to all of them in varying degrees and at various times. The one that will really trip you up will depend on your personal makeup and conditioning.

1. **Arrogance and Inflation**
   Without the frequent influence of a teacher, priest, or other religious authority, there is a danger that you will be blind to your own shadow and to your own weaknesses. You can work with a therapist or counselor, which can be a big help, and it is

advisable to match spiritual development with accompanying psychological work. But ultimately life is our greatest teacher. If you get unhealthily full of yourself, life is sure to bring you a lesson sooner or later to take you down to size. Pay attention to such opportunities!

2. **Laziness and Falling Away from Your Own Path**

   Without a formal practice and an organization to hold you, it is easy to drift off into "normal" secular life and forget about the deep, soul-directed urge that drew you into your spiritual work. For this reason it is a good idea to establish some kind of a regular habit, such as a daily short meditation. This will help keep you centered on the days when mundane life or strong emotion might overwhelm you and distract you from your practice.

3. **Self-doubt**

   It's all too easy on a bad day to think you have been deluding yourself, that your life is a big mess, and that spiritual practice is a pointless indulgence. Again, some kind of regular practice is useful to help stabilize your relationship with yourself and with Spirit. But perhaps more important here is the company of a partner, a close friend, a group of friends, or a therapist — trusted people, spiritual friends, and mentors who know you well and who can remind you who you really are. We all have times when our confidence lags, and one of the best things we can do for our loved ones is offer encouragement and emotional support. Being an independent spiritual practitioner does not mean sacrificing your very human need for close relationship, mutual support, and recognition.

4. **Fear**

   As your consciousness expands, there are likely to be times when your personality gets confused or perturbed. In doing spiritual practice we develop and encounter new levels of perception, and we have to reorient ourselves, much as we do when visiting a foreign land. The unknown territory can provoke fear and anxiety. Rarely, this can be so intense that it causes a break with normal functioning, which is known as a "spiritual emergency." More often, this fear makes itself known as a free-floating anxiety, ready to attach in the moment to any potential hazard.

Fear of the unknown at root invokes our fear of death. The spiritual journey is part of life and allows us to live more fully. It is also a preparation for a conscious and open-hearted death. And while it is natural to fear death, it is also natural to open to the transformation it brings. Spiritual practice can help us be loving to ourselves and to others during our dying so that we leave peacefully rather than in a state of tension and anxiety.

When you go deeply into your own inner process, you will encounter your fear of death. This is inevitably experienced as a challenging initiation, because it causes existential cognitive dissonance: here we are, alive and needing a sense of "I am" to navigate life, and yet we live with the knowledge of our death and "I am not." Once you work your way through this core dilemma and learn to sit peaceably with paradox and the unknown, you encounter bliss, and life never closes down again. You will still experience fears and anxieties, but something in your core will be strengthened in a way that will never leave you.

Taking this part of the journey alone can be difficult, and this is the reason you develop your practices: if you have a practiced, almost automatic relationship with prayer and connection to Spirit, then you won't get so caught by the paralysis that fear can invoke. But if you do get stuck, remember: a good friend, a good book, a spiritual mentor, or a therapist can help you move forward.

# HOW THIS BOOK WORKS

This book is designed to take you through a year of spiritual development with thirteen core lessons. These thirteen lessons give you a solid basis for creating your own spiritual practice and they support your developing awareness of what works for you. Each lesson was created to assist you in deepening your relationship with your inner wisdom and with the unseen forces that guide and protect each and every one of us. By working with this material, you will become more aware of your own journey and thus more centered in your own being, able to easily find strength and sustenance in your relationship with the spiritual realm.

There are thirteen lessons because there are thirteen lunar months in the year. Locating your development in the context of lunar cycles helps ground you in the natural world, one of the lynchpins of a secure independent practice. The idea is that you complete one lesson each lunar month, beginning with the New Moon. You can work faster or slower than this if you want to, but my aim in designing the course has been to anchor this phase of your spiritual development in one solar cycle (a year) and the thirteen lunar cycles within it.

Each lesson contains suggestions for work to do during the month. This homework consists of exercises and practices that will help you ground the information in action and thereby develop your understanding of the territory covered in that month's lesson. The work involved has been completed within a year by many of my students—including people who have full-time jobs and are raising families. It takes some commitment to complete all the lessons, but it is a realistic and workable template for a year's spiritual development.

The intention of this program of study is that by the end of the year you will be much more confident and at home in your personal spiritual reality. The positive ramifications of this centering will have a ripple effect in your life in every dimension.

I recommend that you work on this material quietly and in privacy to begin with. Don't talk about it with other people any more than you absolutely have to. It's about *your* relationship with your own spiritual practice, and it's best to get a firm handle on that before talking about it too much. As the year goes on, if you have a friend engaged in similar work (or perhaps doing the course alongside you), you can begin to share your experiences and support each other.

For each lesson, I've included suggestions for further reading at the back of the book. We are fortunate to live in a period of great creativity—a time that will be looked back on as a genuine renaissance in spiritual literature. This gives us a rapidly growing and readily available collective resource of spiritual texts for the independent practitioner. I've included some of my favorites in this list, but the selection is really just an introduction into the various areas covered in the book. Use it as a springboard and as inspiration for moving forward on your own individual path.

## THE FIRST STEP

The first step in developing an individual spiritual practice, at a practical level, is to make a space in your home that supports you spiritually. In Lesson 1, I'm going to talk about the various elements involved in doing this, and give you a template of actions that you can adapt to your own needs and situation.

The spiritual journey is individual, highly personal.
It can't be organized or regulated. It isn't true that everyone
should follow one path. Listen to your own truth.

—RAM DASS

# Lesson 1

# CREATING SACRED SPACE

◐ ◑ ◯ ◯ ◯ ◑ ◑ ◐ ◐

When you call for blessings and assistance from the
unseen realm of Spirit . . . your house becomes
a home for your soul.
—DENISE LINN, *Space Clearing: How to Purify and
Create Harmony in Your Home*

The knowledge of how to create and foster sacred space is a key
element in the development of an individual spiritual practice.
We can create sacred space anywhere, and historically, human beings
have often chosen to create specific, powerful buildings for this purpose. In this lesson, I focus on creating sacred space in the home, as
this is where we spend much of our time and where we are most likely
to pursue our individual spiritual practice.

There are two elements to this process: first, to clear and bless
the energy of the home itself, and second, to set up a specific area
in the home to pray, meditate, and come to center. The next chapter
explores altar building and creating your area for focused spiritual
practice; this chapter focuses on the fundamental techniques of a
space-clearing ritual for your whole home. Lesson 1 is the entry into
the year's lessons—the beginning, the new year, the spring clean—and
sets you up for the practices to come. This lesson includes detailed
instructions for a thorough cleansing and blessing of your space. If
you prefer a down-to-the-bones approach, feel free to simplify but
maintain the spirit of the actions recommended here.

1

# CLEARING AND BLESSING SPACE

It's necessary to periodically clear the energy of the space we live in—just as we dust and vacuum it on the physical level—because a home that is energetically cluttered won't operate well as a sanctuary and as a healing, restorative space. And if we then invoke blessings by setting our intention and asking for support from the unseen realms, we strengthen the vibrations of the space.

It's much easier to come to center in an atmosphere of peace and harmony, even if our ultimate aim is to be fully awake and centered under any circumstances, anywhere. When our own space nourishes and protects us energetically as well as physically, our spiritual work is aided by the environment we create.

There are two stages in creating sacred space. First you get rid of the old, then you invite in the new. Another way of saying this is to think of purification and blessing.

## PURIFICATION

The first stage is to purify the space from self-negating thought forms and/or old emotionally based energy structures left by yourself or others.

Everything begins with an impulse to create, generated out of the Universal Mind. One way of describing this is to say that everything begins with a thought. In meditation we find that out of a quiet, empty mind, pure thought arises. Clearing out old thought forms and energy structures in one's space allows for new, fresh impulses to occur naturally.

Once you have cleared the energy of the home (or, at the very least, part of the home), you are free to delve into and experience realms of consciousness that are more elusive when one's energy is taken up with coping with external irritants and demands. Of course, irritants and demands are part of life. Embracing and dealing with them is very much part of holistic spiritual and psychological development, but we don't have to be in constant struggle. We can create harmony whenever and wherever possible.

So the first action to take, when you want to either begin your journey or refresh your spiritual practice, is to clear your space of old thoughts and unhelpful energies, bringing the whole space into the present moment, fresh and clear and open to new inspiration.

## BLESSING

The second stage is to bless the space by inviting beneficial energies into it. In this context, there are two types of blessings: those that arise as your own thoughts, and those that are brought by benign and helpful entities. Your thoughts in this case are your prayers and intentions—your wishes for the space. You can either make these prayers and wishes spontaneously or you can prepare by writing them down beforehand. As a general rule, it's a good idea to add "for the highest good" to the end of any prayers in which a request is made.

In terms of benign and helpful entities, there are many ways of looking at this. It's a metaphysical matter, and we all have our own ways of understanding it. My own sense is that we are constantly surrounded by energies ranging from the personal to the archetypal, and these energies are often willing to help us. Some of them seem to help without us asking directly, and other times making a request for assistance appears to be necessary. (There's more about prayer and how we relate to our spiritual guidance later on in the book.)

## TOOLS FOR CREATING SACRED SPACE

The primary tools for creating sacred space are **light/fire**, **aroma**, and **sound**.

These three tools, applied with the intent to purify negativity and to attract benign energies, have been used by cultures all over the world from time immemorial to protect and bless spaces in preparation for ritual and prayer.

From Catholic churches to Tibetan gompas to Japanese temples, you will find the triple technology of fire, aroma, and sound being used to purify the space and the participants, to enable their connection with the sacred.

All these tools are found on or around the altar, and many spiritual practitioners use each of these methods daily.

## 1. Light and Fire

Light is usually supplied by candles in spiritual settings. The flame has always been connected with the spiritual realm for several reasons, not least of which is that life depends upon fire, warmth, and the sun.

In churches and temples all over the world, candles are still lit ritualistically, despite the fact that we now have electric light. Lighting a candle while saying a prayer or making a wish is a universal action. Symbolically, candles represent hope and love, and our connection with the divine. On a metaphysical level, candles make an energetic connection between the individual, the prayer, and unseen forces.

In the Native American tradition, the element of fire is associated with birth, rebirth, the spirit, spiritual teachers, spiritual wisdom, and the direction of the east, the place of the rising sun. The fire that is made to heat the rocks for a sweat lodge is seen as a sacred entity and is always built to the east of the lodge. The rocks are carried into the lodge along a path called the spirit path, which the participants must not cross, as they could disrupt the spiritual energy leading from the fire into the lodge.

Light from candles and fires has a different energy to electric light and creates a very different atmosphere. Simply lighting a candle in a room (especially on an altar) and letting it burn for a while as you sit in contemplation will have the effect of shifting the energy in the room.

Keeping a votive candle lit in a room helps purify the room's energy, especially when the lighting of the candle is accompanied by a prayer. It could be a general prayer for the day or for clearing the space, or a specific request about a current matter or need.

Fire-gazing is a potent method of calming the mind and allowing a gentle altered state to arise. Meditating on the flames is an initiation into the essence of inspiration. Outdoor fires are particularly wonderful for this, if you can make one safely.

2. **Aroma**

Aroma is supplied by several methods. One method is the burning of herbs, such as sage, cedar, and lavender. In the Native American tradition, these herbs are called smudge, and the act of burning them and then wafting the smoke over people or spaces with a feather is called smudging. Traditionally, an abalone shell is used to burn smudge in. Sometimes the herbs are tied together with cord to form a thick, long wand called a smudge stick. The end of the stick is lit and used to waft and direct the smoke. The smudge stick can be used with a smudging feather, traditionally an eagle feather, but any large feather will work.

Burning incense is another popular method. There are two main ways to do this: burning resins such as copal or frankincense on top of charcoal or, more commonly, using stick or cone incense, which is a more controllable way of burning herbs and resins.

Essential oils can be used in a custom heater or as a room spray. You can find such oils in health food stores and specialty outlets. The scent from aromatic flowers or leaves such as roses or eucalyptus is also a pleasing, accessible way to purify and bless a space.

If you share your home, make sure your cohabitants are not allergic to certain smells or smoke. Sometimes allergy-prone people find the smoke from incense worsens their symptoms, in which case essential oils or aromatic flowers may be preferable.

In the Native American tradition there is a sophisticated understanding of the effects different herbs and resins have on the energy of the space and on the people within it. Sage clears negative energy; cedar brings wisdom (grandfather energy); lavender brings beauty and harmony (feminine energy); copal (a resin used in Central America) opens the third eye and thus aids inner vision.

Traditional knowledge about herbs, resins, and flowers tells us what to use for different situations. Advancements in the study of essential oils in recent years have added to our knowledge of the effects of different plants, and there are many great books on essential oils and their properties.

## 3.  Sound

Sound includes both live and recorded sound. Singing, chanting, and drumming are powerful ways to claim a space and break up and eject unwanted energies. Music is one of the prime ways human beings connect with the ineffable.

Drumming, especially with a ritual drum made for performing ceremonies, breaks up negative thought forms and old, accumulated energies. It is a highly effective method for space clearing.

Tibetan singing bowls have reputedly been used since the time of the Buddha in the fifth century BC. Made of a twelve-metal alloy, singing bowls create sounds that are immediately centering and have an instant impact on brain activity, generating a meditative state of mind. It is claimed that they balance left/right brain synchronization. In my experience they not only calm and balance the brain but also the vibrations of the room. It is really worth investing in a good singing bowl, whether you get an antique Tibetan metal bowl, a small Japanese bowl, or one of the new crystal bowls available.

Singing purifies space when it's the kind of singing that opens the throat and heart chakras, and shifts consciousness.

Feel the room and then allow yourself to make free-form vocalizations, opening the throat fully and breathing deeply into your lungs. This is the open-singing technique.

Chanting has a powerful effect on spaces and is an important aid to centering and spiritual development. When you use the open-singing technique, you may find that you naturally chant certain sounds, such as "Aaaah" or "Ohmmm."

Wind chimes, angel chimes, rattles, and small Druid bells are all potent methods of using sound to purify space and welcome transformative energies. Rattles are also great for shaking out old energy and awakening the new. Druid bells are especially magical for lightening mood and taking you into a pure, childlike, angelic state of wonder.

Playing CDs and tapes also helps to set the atmosphere, soothe jangled nerves, and clear spaces. There's a great deal of inspiring music on the market these days, ranging from ancient Egyptian music to gravelly Tibetan chanting to oceanic dolphin sounds. Websites often have music samples and many stores have listening stations, so you can listen and find out what you like before making a purchase. For suggestions about where to purchase spiritually inspiring music, see the resources section at the end of this book.

## ADDITIONAL ELEMENTS IN CREATING SACRED SPACE

There are many other ingredients that help create sacred space and that are found cross-culturally. It's important to pay attention to the aesthetic dimension of your space and to be mindful of everything you place within it. Items from the natural world, especially crystals and water, are nature's cleansers and purifiers, so beauty, crystals, and water are all ways to enhance your space. Feel free to add any others you can think of.

## BEAUTY

An essential part of the creation of sacred space is respect for beauty
and form. In most cultures, art is found in religious spaces, and often
the grandest buildings are those devoted to spiritual worship. Beautiful flower arrangements grace churches and cathedrals. Japanese
temples are masterpieces of grace and simplicity both inside the buildings and in the grounds.

In the feng shui tradition there is a detailed appreciation of form
as an integral aspect of spiritual harmony. This aspect will come into
play when you build an altar (or rebuild your existing one) in Lesson
2. But if there is anything in your space that strikes you as ugly or
offensive, now is a good time to get rid of it.

## CRYSTALS

Crystals have many functions. They are beautiful, they subtly shift
awareness, and they stimulate energy movement when placed on or
near the body. Many practitioners consider that crystals have the
capacity to absorb negative vibrations, especially from modern electri-
cal appliances. Crystals are one of the tools we can use when clearing
and blessing a space.

The most effective crystal for cleansing is clear quartz. This is the
best broad-spectrum crystal, and it has a wide range of applications.
Other crystals are used to bless the space and influence the energy in
specific ways. For example, amethyst is both purifying and calming and
acts as a bridge energy between different levels of consciousness, helping us access spiritual information. Another useful crystal is rose quartz,
which opens the heart, helps us give and receive more love, and can be
very appropriate when blessing a space in the home.

You can choose crystals by reading a book on them and deciding
from that information which ones you need, and/or you can choose
your crystals intuitively. Go to a crystal store and slowly walk around,
noticing which crystals your body is drawn to and which ones your
hand just reaches out and picks up. Choose the ones you are attracted
to—ones that you like the shape of and that feel good to you when

you hold them in your hand. There is also a lot of quartz freely available in nature, so when you are out hiking, keep an eye out for any suitable stones and chunks of quartz that catch your eye.

To use your crystals, place them somewhere in the room, preferably close to any area that you feel needs cleansing or protection (for example, next to a computer or on a windowsill to protect the boundary of your space). They can stay there all the time, acting as a constant source of subtle energy balancing and as beautiful, light-reflecting objects in their own right.

Because crystals absorb energy, they need to be cleaned regularly. There are several ways of doing this. The easiest way to clean crystals is to leave them in a bowl of salt water overnight and then rinse them off in the morning, drying them carefully. You can also clean them by placing them in the light of the full moon for several hours, by putting them in sunlight, or by rinsing them in the ocean.

I was taught to clean my crystals by a Mayan shaman, a man in his eighties who had been working with crystals since he was a small child. He showed me how to take the crystals to the ocean on the night of a full moon, hold them in the ocean for several minutes, and then hold them up so that the rays of the moon shone through them.

These days I don't live by the ocean, so I put my crystals in a bowl filled with salt water overnight and then leave them in the sunlight for the day. Once a year I give them a full moon treatment at the ocean. You can create your own cleansing ritual for your crystals. The act of taking care of your crystals can be very centering and soothing.

## WATER

Water is the ultimate solvent and the best cleanser. Salt water is very useful in purification. In particularly clogged atmospheres, you can do a salt-water treatment by sprinkling salt water throughout the house. You can also use holy water from a sacred river or spring, or water that a spiritual teacher has blessed. If you don't have any holy water, bless the water yourself, acknowledging the water spirits

of your water supply and asking for their cleansing powers to help
you in your ritual.

## SPACE-CLEARING AND BLESSING RITUAL

Beginning your ritual in a clean house will greatly add to its success.
So before you start the ritual, clean the space on a physical level.
Sweep, vacuum, dust, and polish all surfaces and clean the windows.
Even though you might not find housecleaning an uplifting pursuit,
research shows that after doing mundane tasks, we secrete higher
amounts of endorphins, the hormones that bring a sense of pleasure
to mind and body.

Make sure you do the ritual at a time when you won't be disturbed. Turn the phone off. If you have family or friends who would
like to participate and you would like them to join you, feel free to
include them in your ritual.

You may also want to eat lightly that day and save your main meal
for after you have completed the ritual. Most spiritual work goes better on a fairly empty stomach.

First of all, get organized. Collect together the tools you think you
may want to use for the ritual: sage and other herbs; an abalone shell;
a feather; a drum and other instruments like rattles, bells, and singing
bowls; salt water and/or holy water; and candles. To make it easier, it's
a good idea to put them all in a box or basket so you have ready
access and aren't interrupting your ritual by having to hunt for things
you have mislaid in another room.

Next, as with all rituals, cleanse your own energy field. I like to
use smudge to do this—usually sage and cedar, but you can use any
smudge stick you like as long as it has some sage in it. If you don't live
in an area where those plants are easily found, buy some loose sage
and burn it in a fireproof bowl, preferably an abalone shell. Use your
feather to scoop up the smoke from the burning herbs, and brush the
smoke through your energy field. If you don't want to use smudge,
you can use incense in a similar way, or you can sprinkle holy water

or salt water over yourself. Some people are allergic to smudge and incense, and prefer to use other cleansing methods. If you have no physical cleansing methods available or if you cannot use what is available, you can use visualization to see your energy cleansed.

After you have cleansed your energy field, close your eyes and imagine yourself surrounded by a gentle golden light of protection and illumination. (This is a universally applicable way of imagining inspiration and protection, but if you have another one you prefer, feel free to use it instead.)

Stand at the threshold of the room (or at the main entrance and then at the doorway of each room if you are clearing a whole house or apartment) and take a few minutes or more to feel out the atmosphere. Perhaps the room already feels quite clear and joyful. Or perhaps it has always been a space that has not quite worked for you, and has felt unhappy or cloudy in some way. Let yourself tune in, and ask yourself what the energy of the room is telling you about what it needs.

Once you have a sense of the room, pick out the tools from your box that you want to use for the clearing and blessing of the space. Do this with the feeling of the room in your mind, so that you let yourself be intuitively drawn to pick up the things you need. If you get an intuitive sense that you need something unanticipated, go get it. One time I did a major space clearing, and I had no idea I would need salt as much as I did, but I found myself in the kitchen with a large jar of salt in my hand.

The next step is to light a candle in the room. Choose a candle that will burn for a while and that is safely held in a heat-proof container. If the candle is scented, make sure it is a scent you like and that goes with the vibration of the room.

Walk around the room with your cleansing/clearing tools (e.g., drum, smudge, salt water), paying particular attention to any area that draws you or feels particularly sticky energetically—to nooks and crannies and corners. Sticky places tend to be hard to clean or frequently get cluttered with stuff. They may have an atmosphere of faint neglect. When you are doing the space-clearing ritual, you'll find yourself literally stuck in these places, unable to clearly move on until you have cleansed the space. If smudging doesn't do the trick, try drumming.

As you walk, say your intention for the space out loud. If this is the first time you have cleansed the space and/or it feels especially clogged (for example, after an argument, a difficult visitor, or an illness or trauma), focus the first round of prayers on asking for purification, release, and letting go. If you feel there are any lingering energies in the room, request that they leave. Break up pockets of old, stale, frustrated energy by drumming right into them. Let yourself go into your intuition here; don't second-guess your body and your immediate thoughts. If you find yourself obsessively banging the drum in one corner, just carry on until the energy shifts. You'll feel it when it does.

Then go around the room again, stating your intention for the room, saying prayers for what you would like to experience in the room, and asking for any blessings you wish for. Express your gratitude for the room and for having this space in which to do (x) or (y). For example, when blessing the bedroom, set the intention for restorative sleep, clear dreams, good health, and loving relations. In the kitchen, set the intention for healthy meals, abundant food, strong nourishment, happiness in the work of cooking and cleaning, and fun and sharing with loved ones.

In each room, and in each part of each room, you are telling yourself what you want this room to help you with in your life. If it feels right for you, you can make a protective shape in the air with your smudge stick or crystal, or simply your hand. For example, you can draw a pentagram (a five-pointed star and an ancient symbol of protection) in each of the corners of the room and one again in the center. You can also do an infinity symbol, a heart, a Sanskrit seed syllable such as "Om," or any simple sign that means something positive to you.

When you feel you have finished clearing and blessing your space, it is time to dedicate the merit of your ritual to all beings. This is a Buddhist tradition that I find very helpful. It's an important recognition that every act we take has an influence on the world around us and that we can have no idea of how far that influence may extend. At the close of every ritual, we say thanks to all the energies that have helped us, and we offer up the beneficial outcome of our practice to all beings.

With all that energy stirred up, it's a good idea to clear your own energy field at this point. Take a shower and rub your body with a mixture of sea salt and a few drops of lavender oil. If you can't shower for some reason, a good smudging will do.

Once you have cleared and blessed your home or room, keep it that way by burning smudge and essential oils, lighting candles, and playing healing music on a regular basis. Whenever it feels necessary, do a deeper energy cleanse on the room or rooms.

When a space is clear, it feels brighter. This is tangible. Even if you don't feel it now, you will feel it the next time you walk into the room or into the house from outside. Doing this ritual can have a much stronger effect than you might think, and it has the capacity to promote major beneficial life changes. You are making a clear statement about your positive intentions in the present moment, and this gives a wonderful opportunity for starting fresh and unblocking previously clogged areas in your life. It's a great thing to do at the beginning of the year and a great way to begin this course of lessons.

## PROBLEMATIC SPACES: WHAT TO DO IF THE ENERGY STILL FEELS WEIRD

Our environments are full of thoughts, full of the energy left by thought forms that have been generated by ourselves, by others who inhabit our spaces with us, and by those who have lived there before. Sometimes these thought forms persist in a particularly strong form, and then they appear more like an entity than a thought. At one end of the energy continuum, it is very flimsy and mutable, and at the other it is more defined. At a certain point of aggregation, energy becomes more fixed into the realm of substance.

From a shamanic perspective, the idea of unhelpful entities being in one's space is philosophically contiguous with the concept that invisible realms are part of reality. The reality we can't see with our everyday vision is part of the overall worldview of shamanic cultures. The main role of the shaman is to act as a go-between for the visible and invisible realms. Sometimes this means they need to help entities that are unable to move on without assistance.

Usually purifying a space is not hard to do. On very rare occasions, extra assistance is needed to clear a particularly troubled space. Often, simply having one or two people help is sufficient. A friend of mine moved into a house that had pretty strange energy, and four of us did a ritual to break up the energy and move it out. We used many of the techniques I've described, including a lot of purposeful drumming and the opening of windows to expel troubling vibrations. It worked.

Another time, I was staying in a motel while at a conference in Oregon. The first night, I couldn't sleep and lay awake with the strangest sensation that I was lying on top of a pile of dead bodies. In the morning I told someone about it, and he said, "Oh yes, this place was built against much local protest because it's on an Indian burial ground." That day I did a ceremony with a friend, acknowledging the spirits of the area, apologizing for the insult done to them, and requesting that we be left in peace while we stayed there. From then on, the room felt peaceful and I slept fine.

One of the key ingredients in clearing spaces in this way is to move beyond superstitious fear about the dead and the unseen. Any energies around are not so different from you; they just don't have a body right now. You can communicate with them, and it's actually the job of anyone with a shamanic-type process (which includes many spiritual seekers) to help spirits who are stuck or lost.

## COLLECTIVE SACRED SPACE

Sometimes people who follow an unconventional spiritual path feel uncomfortable in the homes of more traditional religious worship.

Sometimes we think that we have no right to take solace in the beauty of religious buildings when we have rejected the whole package.

Yet those buildings were created to foster that sense of solace in beauty and of wonder at the vastness of Spirit. The builders of the great cathedrals and temples were artists, first and foremost, who understood the relationship of space and form to love and awe. They were not necessarily dogmatic religionists. And if you drop down and tune in to the energy of these great buildings—in all religious traditions—you can feel that at root, all religions have the same message: love, awe, and devotion to the whole.

I encourage you to visit collective sacred spaces—from cathedrals and mosques to stone circles and ancient wells—and to absorb the deep resonance of devotion and care that exists within these structures. Pilgrimages to sacred places can inspire us and move us along on our individual journey. When you visit these places, add your blessings and prayers to the mix, even if you do not officially belong to the religion of the place. In the world of Spirit, all is one.

---

## WHAT TO DO THIS MONTH

If you don't already have the items you need for the sacred space ritual, do the relevant shopping. Then find a time to do your clearing and blessing ritual.

Establish a daily habit of lighting a candle and some incense or smudge, and playing some kind of sacred sounds in your room.

The next lesson is about altar building. Begin gathering items that you think you might want to have on your altar. If you have an altar already, see what objects your eye lights upon to consider adding to your altar in the coming month.

# Lesson 2
## MAKING ALTARS

● ◐ ○ ○ ◑ ● ●

The altar is a powerful tool for rooting life in meaning.
—LAURA CERWINSKE, *In a Spiritual Style: The Home as Sanctuary*

Once you have purified and blessed your room or rooms, the next step in creating sacred space is to make an altar. If you already have an altar, use this lesson as stimulus to deepen your relationship with it and maybe add to or change it in some way. Or you may wish to make a new one in another part of your home.

Having an altar is a very effective way to integrate the sacred into your everyday life. An altar is one of the prime ingredients in sacred space and acts as a focal point for your spiritual intent. It is a physical place in your home devoted solely to the representation of Spirit.

The creation of a part of your home, however small, reserved for spiritual practice and focus, is a fundamental step in respecting both the personal context of your own spiritual life and the larger context of the spirit that infuses everything, the Source.

People have always made altars. Creating a special place for ritual, prayer, ceremony, and reflection is part of the human story. For many years in Western society, altars, for the most part, existed only inside churches or synagogues, and held sacred objects such as the cross, the Bible or the Torah, and statues and candles. But a shift in consciousness has been occurring since the 1960s, influenced by indigenous traditions and Asian religions. This shift goes along with a sense that God / the sacred doesn't live solely in the church or temple but lives within our own homes. This changed sense of God's location is represented by the increasing number of people who have altars in their homes and who find spiritual sustenance from creating a sense of the sacred in their own houses. The church has moved from the town square and into our bedrooms and living rooms. We can each create sacred space.

## WHAT IS AN ALTAR?

In mainstream Western religious tradition, altars are found in churches and temples.

In the East, you find little altar tables everywhere—in houses, in gardens, and on the street—with pictures of deities, vases of flowers, statues of gods and goddesses, and other artifacts. In recent years, as more and more people have been influenced by the more spontaneous and creative Eastern traditions, people in the West have also started creating their own altars at home as a focus of their spiritual life. This trend is especially apparent among people claiming an independent relationship with their spiritual life. The concept of the altar has developed along with a growing sense of the divine being within as well as without, and existing everywhere, not just in a church or temple.

In this context, your altar is a place in your home and/or garden where you go to find spiritual nourishment and solace. It is a spiritual "safe space," a place where you can be peaceful and rest your eyes on objects of spiritual beauty and meaning. It is a focus for spiritual practice, in front of which we can remind ourselves of our divine origins and ask for guidance, give thanks, and open up to spiritual wisdom.

When I first made an altar, sometime in the early 1980s, it felt like hubris to call it an altar, and for a while I hedged and called it my special table. I was in my twenties, and the idea of independent spiritual practice was new to me. I had been raised in the Church of England, and to call my special table an altar felt sacrilegious. I was afraid that people might think I was getting a bit above myself, thinking that I could have an altar in my own home.

But the need to have a focus for my spiritual practice was a very strong and clear desire. I was chiefly inspired by Buddhism, and the practice of having an altar in the home was considered quite normal in that context. This helped get me over the notion that there was a split between the holy place and the home.

I put things on the table that I had been carrying around with me for years: a little statue of a Chinese sage I had had since I was sixteen and a few things I had collected on my travels, as well as the usual candles and incense. Gradually I collected artifacts especially for the table.

People, without knowing about my altar, began giving me presents that were perfect for it. A friend who was a Buddhist monk gave me a little statue of Quan Yin, the Chinese goddess of compassion. My mother gave me a beautiful little porcelain dish that became a water bowl on the altar. One of my colleagues gave me an amethyst crystal. After a while I became less self-conscious, and when visitors asked, "What's that?" I would say with growing ease, "That's my altar."

I developed a practice of sitting in front of my altar at some point during the day, usually in the morning, lighting a candle and some incense, and meditating and saying prayers. Since then I have always had at least one altar in my home and often one in each room. Over the years they have changed, had different themes, and have been more or less elaborate, but the basic desire that the altar reflect back to me the values of peace, beauty, and wisdom has remained the same.

Times have changed since I first made my foray into altar building. Ideas from feng shui have permeated the mainstream, and Buddhism has continued to exert a big influence on Western spiritual practice. These days lots of people have altars, and it's not really such an unusual thing to do anymore. If you are new to the idea and were raised in a traditional Western religion, you may feel a little weird about your altar at first, as I did, but don't worry; that feeling won't last.

## WHY HAVE AN ALTAR?

An altar is a sacred place you create in your own home to express your spirituality. It is a place to sit in front of and center yourself, to meditate, and to pray. It is a place to receive guidance and wisdom. A home altar allows you to blend your creativity and spirituality as you create and look after it, using it to reflect your spiritual changes and development.

People who have altars are often people who want to express their spirituality in their own unique way. They may not relate to mainstream religions, or they may wish to augment their church- or temple-going activities with a personal altar.

I suggest you create an altar of your own so that you can nourish yourself spiritually in everyday life; in seeing your altar daily, you will see that what is holy is not separate from your intimate, domestic, everyday reality. Nourishing your soul in everyday life means staying in touch with your connection to the divine. The most simple, effective way to do this is through the very physical manifestation of this desire in the form of a tangible creation—your altar.

## CREATING YOUR ALTAR

An altar is a form of spiritual art. It might be changed the next day or it might stay as it is for several months. You can make a new altar as often as you like to symbolize and envision whatever aspect of life you wish to express or deepen into. You can also have permanent altars that you only change when a major transition occurs; or you may have a fundamental altar design that you like and that feels centering to you, keeping it the same way for several years or even decades.

Your altar is your personal and creative expression of your rela-tionship with the sacred. Please take my suggestions as just that—

suggestions—and feel utterly free to make your altar in the style that feels right for you.

Your altar is an ideal place for your most meaningful personal items and power objects. We all collect talismans over the course of our lives. Even if they don't seem overtly spiritual, if they have a deep meaning for you, they may well belong on your altar. For example, I was in the hospital many years ago, and some close friends came to visit with their son, a little boy I knew and loved very much. He brought me a present: a little plastic card that read, "Be Kind to Monsters," with a picture of a monster's face on it. This card has lived on one of my altars ever since, a message to me to be kind even when I am repelled or afraid.

The things we carry around with us for years absorb our energy and become our personal power objects, even though they may not have any apparent sacred value to anyone else. You may have something—a little ornament, a keepsake, or your grandmother's locket—that holds a certain precious energy for you. Think about placing these items on your altar as part of creating a beautiful, meaningful arrangement of personalized spiritual art.

I also have more predictable precious items on my altars, such as an antique Tibetan singing bowl, a Buddha, a painting of the Buddhist deity Tara, photographs of my spiritual teachers, and a statue of a meditating woman.

I keep those precious things that are not currently in use in an altar box that I place somewhere near my bed so that it will absorb my energy and nourish me. Every now and then, when I redo an altar, I consult the box to see if it has anything that fits with the design and theme of the new altar.

## WHERE TO PUT YOUR ALTAR

The location of your altar is important because you need to feel comfortable putting whatever you want on the altar, and you need to be able to sit there in peace and solitude. Don't censor yourself for other people. Bedrooms are good places for altars because that is where you are often the most free to be yourself.

But if you share a bedroom, it may not work to have your altar there, depending on how your partner feels. You may feel it will work better if you find a private space somewhere else in the house. This can be a bit of a problem and can take some domestic negotiation. It is often especially problematic for men because they may not be practiced in claiming domestic space for themselves. If you share a home and have a personal office/study, this may be the best place for your altar. You can also create a shared altar if this suits you as a couple and/or family.

## THE ALTAR BASE

For the base of your altar, it's best to use a table or chest that is about chest height when you are seated on a cushion on the floor. That way, the artifacts and pictures on your altar are easily visible and work for you when you are sitting down. If you can't sit on the floor, make the table the right height to sit in front of it comfortably on a chair.

## BASIC TEMPLATE FOR CREATING ALTARS

The design of an altar is largely a matter of personal taste. Some people like Zen/Protestant altars—bare, stark, white, simple, open, and calming. Others are in the more flamboyant Tibetan/Catholic stream—bright colors, lots of stuff, metal, beads, icons, and images. Then there's the Native American / pagan altar style, which largely features the natural world—stones, shells, bits of animal skins, and feathers. Personally, I favor a mix of the Tibetan and the Native American / pagan styles, so this lesson is rather influenced by my own preferences. Please adjust your altar to your own style. If your happiest sense of an altar is a white cloth with one candle on it, please go ahead with it.

The many models and styles of altars all over the world have their own symbols and designs, yet they usually contain the following basic ingredients.

## COLOR

Color is important to think about because color itself conveys a mood and message. The colors of your altar can soothe or stimulate you; they can help you feel centered and well. Red is good for grounding and warming, and for creating passion and energy. Gold and yellow awaken, and they are great for generating feelings of joy, happiness, abundance, and expansion. Blue creates a calm, deep, reflective atmosphere. Green stimulates healing emotions and thoughts, and connects us with the energy of nature. White creates an atmosphere of purity and quiet. Purple is a powerful color with a strong and majestic energy. Pink gives feelings of warmth, loving kindness, and pleasure. Combining colors creates different effects. Follow your instincts with color and go for what attracts you.

The chief ways you can incorporate color into your altar are through altar cloths, crystals, flowers/plants, and candles. For example, at one stage I had an altar that was chiefly pink, cream, and white, with a rose-patterned altar cloth, rose quartz crystals, and white candles. The focus of that altar was loving kindness and peaceful contemplation. Another altar was focused on right action and prosperity. It lived in my office and was colored purple, gold, and red, and had a large amethyst in the center; fat, round, golden-yellow candles on Indian brass dishes; and silken red and gold cloths.

These are just a couple of ideas for your altar, but the possibilities are infinite. Use color as an artist would when you are creating your altar: go for what fills your heart with joy and looks beautiful to you.

## IMAGES AND ICONS

Using collective images is a powerful way to give your altar depth of meaning and link you to archetypal energies. Images you might want to use include pictures or sculptures of deities, wise beings, and spiritual teachers; pictures of the earth from outer space; photographs of natural sites such as mountains, rivers, or oceans; pictures of animals, birds, or other beings that possess qualities you would like to incorporate; and symbols such as spirals, hearts, or stars. These images or figurines help you center, meditate, and pray. They represent the qualities, values, and attitudes you cherish in life and wish to cultivate.

Personal images may also have a place on your altar. It can be very powerful to place a favorite photograph of yourself on your altar. It makes a literal connection between you and the sacred. If you are working on self-love or feel in need of help, a photo of yourself that you like can enhance your self-appreciation in a non-narcissistic way. Put the photo of yourself next to one of a spiritual teacher you admire, and you'll feel their protection and support. This is a kind of sympathetic magic that works in times of difficulty, and it is a good practice at any time, as it links you to positive qualities in your mind. Whenever you look at the altar, you'll see yourself in proximity to someone warm, wise, and calm. It will rub off! Choose photographs that express the aspect of yourself you want to connect with more fully. You can use a photograph of you looking strong, happy, or peaceful. You can also use a photograph of yourself as a child to help connect you to your most fundamental qualities, your core quest in life, and your soul essence.

Pictures of ancestors and descendants can help us feel part of a greater unbroken chain of life, and unconditionally loved and supported. However, I would like to add a word of caution here about adding family photos: Don't feel that you have to represent all your loved ones on your altar. Put some photographs somewhere else in the house, or have a separate mini-altar for photos of loved ones. I keep my main altar space for pictures of very wise beings only. I've known people, usually women, who felt they were somehow being disloyal to their family if they didn't put all of them on the altar. Remember, your altar should exist as a place to nourish you to start with. It is a *personal* resource.

If you do place a picture of someone on your altar, make sure that it is someone who respects you and who would respect your altar. Your altar should be a place in your life before which you feel unequivocally supported.

## MEDITATION TOOLS

Your altar can be a home for the aids you need to support your meditation/contemplation practice, such as candles, incense, malas/prayer beads, Tibetan bowls, and bells. I'll talk about these aids in more detail in the meditation section of the book, Lesson 5. You may already have such things, and you have the tools you used in the space-clearing ritual—some version of light/fire, scent/incense, and sound. That's a good start.

## THE FOUR ELEMENTS

Some representation of the elements is commonly found on altars. There are four elements in the Celtic and Native American traditions and five in Tibetan and Chinese traditions. For now let's keep it simple and use four.

Integrating the elements into your altar is a way of bringing in the natural world. This both grounds the altar (and, by extension, your spiritual practice) and honors the world we live in. All of nature has value and spiritual significance, and these four elements represent the basic structure of life. Each element possesses a specific meaning and has its own symbols and associations.

**Fire** = The Spiritual Realm, represented by candles and the colors red or gold

**Earth** = The Physical Realm, represented by herbs; plants; rocks; earth (dirt); cornmeal; and the colors yellow, green, or black

**Air** = The Mental Realm, represented by feathers and crystals, and the colors white or light/sky blue

**Water** = The Emotional Realm, represented by a bowl of water (or holy water); seashells; and the color blue, red, or green

Having the four elements represented on your altar creates a feeling of wholeness and completion. It also serves as a reminder that you are a part of the greater whole.

## ALTAR DESIGNS

Here are a couple of suggested altar designs based on two different traditions. You can use them as a starting point, combine them, or model your altar on one of them entirely if that feels right to you.

### THE FOUR DIRECTIONS ALTAR

In classic Native American tradition, air is linked with the direction of north, fire with east, water with south, and earth with west. You can lay out items relating to the elements in the place of their direction on your table, being literal and putting them in the true directions, or you can simply make the far side of the table north and the side nearest you south.

Air is commonly represented by feathers. You can place a feather or a picture of a bird in the north or you can use some other object that represents air to you, such as an angel or a star image. Crystals also belong to this element. Air is the home of mental clarity and the capacity to have an overview. Pictures of people who have this quality can go here, too. The color white also represents air, so you can place a white object here as well.

Earth is represented by cornmeal (or another grain representing the fruit of the earth) or actual soil—the literal earth itself. You can also use a plant or a rock in this position. In the Native American tradition, west is the place of woman, fertility, magic, mystery, healing, and death and transformation. You can use anything here that symbolizes for you the transformative power of female energy, such as a goddess figurine or a mythological entity associated with the feminine. The color black is another option, as it represents the quality of earth and the direction of west.

Fire is represented by fire itself, so here we use candles. The east is the home of spiritual wisdom and the masculine, and hence of the wise man, so a picture of a sage or spiritual teacher can go here. The colors gold or yellow represent the fire element and the east.

For water in the south, the home of feelings, you can use a small bowl of water. Shells are good here, as is anything that reminds you of children, trust, innocence, and the spirit of play. The color red represents the south. Green is also associated with this direction.

In the center of the altar, you can place any power objects you own. Then light your candle in the east, fill your water bowl in the south, touch the earth in the west, and feel the clarifying energy of the crystal in the north. As you meditate at your altar, feel which direction is speaking to you at this time, and allow the wisdom of the natural world to teach you and infuse you.

## THE CHAKRA ALTAR

The chakra system is an ancient Indian concept of energy vortices in the body that has found much favor in contemporary spirituality. The chakra altar design gives us a visual and energetic representation of our own subtle energy body. Sitting at this altar helps clarify our sense of our own embodiment and how it is functioning for us at different levels of density and awareness.

For this design, you need crystals in the colors of each chakra. Place them in a design as if they were the chakras of your body: red at the bottom nearest you for the base chakra; then above that, orange for the second, sacral chakra; yellow for the solar plexus chakra; green for the heart chakra (you can use pink here, too); turquoise for the throat; indigo for the third eye; and violet and/or white/clear for the crown chakra located at the top of the head.

If you feel drawn to add more crystals, incorporate them into the basic template for the design. This altar can become a colorful and vibrant healing space, and it is a good way to develop your understanding of subtle healing energies. Crystals are attractive, and creating a beautiful crystal design on your altar can make the altar space more appealing, encouraging you to come and sit and find your peaceful center.

You can add this design into the Four Directions design by surrounding the crystals with the representations of the four elements and with your power objects. This is a strengthening altar arrangement for your own energy field and is particularly appropriate when you are going through a lot of change and upheaval.

## STEPS TO CREATE YOUR ALTAR

There are two ways to do this: You can start making your altar and design it as you go, using the energy of the moment, your instincts, and your intuition to guide you. Or, if you like to plan ahead and/or if this is your first altar, you can do the following process to help you begin designing it in your mind.

If you already have an altar, you can use this exercise to see if there are some changes you want to make and to discover additional information from your imagination.

Sit down with a pen and paper. Take a few deep breaths, feel your feet on the floor, and let your imagination lead you.

1. First of all, think about how you want your altar to be. In your mind's eye, allow an image of your altar to arise. Is it peaceful, calm, and contemplative, or festive, colorful, and expressive? What is the general sense or atmosphere of your altar? Is it in a private or public part of your home? Do you want more than one altar? Some people find they have a big altar process and create one for each room.

2. Make some notes about this vision. Now that you have a general sense of your altar, fill in the details. Make notes at each step as you go through this process.

3. How big do you want your altar to be? Do you want it to be big and dramatic or small and simple? Some altars are large and house many objects, becoming a central feature in a room. Others are tiny and relatively unnoticeable.

4. Where will you put your altar? In what part of the house would you like it to be? Ideally, your altar will be easy for you

to use on a regular basis as a resource for contemplation. But if this isn't possible, you can get around it by putting the altar in a closet and pulling it out when needed. I know of one woman who made her altar on a tray and kept it under the bed. She slid it out whenever she wanted to use it.

5. What will you use as the altar base? You can, of course, use existing shelves or mantelpieces. But for sitting in front of the altar and meditating, you need to find a low table or something similar. A robust cardboard box can work fine, as can a packing case or trunk. For my main altar, I use an antique pine blanket chest that I have had for many years and have kept through many house moves. I have other altars in a deep bay window, various windowsills and mantelpieces, and on shelves.

6. When you close your eyes, what colors do you see? Are they bold and colorful or soft and muted? Does passionate red dominate or cool blue? Do you see lots of gold or gentle pinks? Is the vision mostly white, signifying purity, or full of majestic purples? Remember that you will probably want to change the colors at some time to reflect your own energy or the season, so just let yourself go with whatever comes into your mind now. It's not a lifetime commitment! You can easily change the color scheme of an altar with scarves, cloths, candles, pictures, and flowers.

7. What do you have already that you'd like to put on the altar? You probably already possess items that hold significance for you. Let your mind travel through your possessions. What do you own that holds special meaning for you? Here are some things commonly found on altars: candleholders; incense holders; (small) vases for flowers; pictures or figurines of deities; pictures or items of natural beauty like shells, stones, crystals, jewels; and bowls for salt, rice, or water.

8. Do you need to buy something new for your altar? Does it need a picture or statuette of a favorite deity or spiritual teacher? How about special candles or incense? Perhaps it

needs a silk scarf to cover the table or box you are using as
the base. Once again, let your imagination roam and see what
your altar needs to be complete.

9.  How does it feel in your body when you think about making
    an altar? As you contemplate the look of your altar and your
    relationship to it in daily life, see how you feel in your body.
    Whatever the feeling is, just notice it. Your altar can be a pow-
    erful way to access certain feelings in your life. Each time you
    see it or even think of it, your altar can shift your conscious-
    ness or your feelings and help you feel more centered, secure,
    and in contact with yourself and your innate wisdom.

## CREATING A PORTABLE ALTAR

There are times in life when we do a lot of traveling and can't be close
to our altar at home. A portable altar is a great way to maintain your
practices and create a sacred space wherever you go.

I spent one year traveling almost continually, and I created a
portable altar from a small bag of various items. There was a small
candle in a holder, a tiny bag of sage and a little shell to burn it on, a
lighter, a mala (prayer beads), a tiny statue of the Buddha, a photograph of one of my spiritual teachers, a couple of crystals, a couple of
magical (to me) things I had had for many years, a little bag of cornmeal for blessings and offerings, and a cloth to put them all on.

Whenever I arrived at a new place, the first thing I did was set up
my little altar in my room. I found it very comforting and centering,
and it provided a spiritual home for me, no matter where I was.

## MAINTAINING YOUR ALTAR

1.  Use your altar often. Keep your altar alive by using it in your
    life regularly. This can range from developing a daily medita-
    tion practice of sitting at your altar to simply gazing at it
    from time to time during the day, taking in its beauty. Walk
    to your altar, sit down, and breathe deeply for a moment. Let
    your altar nourish you.

2.  Keep your altar dusted and fresh. Nurture it. Don't let your altar take on a neglected or dusty look. Take the time to freshen it up. Dust it or change something about it. Put some fresh flowers on it or burn some incense. Change the color of the candles or put a new figurine on it. Buy beautiful items for the altar now and then. Over time, slowly build up the power of your altar and the power of the objects on it by giving them your attention.

3.  Enjoy your altar. An altar should be beautiful and calming, and you should feel proud and happy when you look at it. Enjoy this island of spiritual support in your life.

## THE EVOLVING ALTAR

Once you build your altar, you will notice that it evolves over time, just as you do. It's a creative space and reflects the moods and events in your life. Don't turn your altar into a relic. Let it live and change and develop. By keeping it current, you are also keeping current with your own spiritual life. You are continuously expressing what's important for you.

Keeping your altar current needn't take more than a few minutes a week. For instance, place a single flower in a cup, change a few pictures, remove or replace an item, or change a candle. It's that simple. What you do with your altar is very personal and will evolve over time.

As your outer life changes and as your inner life shifts in emphasis, your altar will change to reflect these shifts. Sometimes making a radical change to your altar presages a life change because the unconscious often prepares us for change through our creative acts, as well as through our dreams and intuitions.

Follow your inner promptings about your altar. If you find yourself bored or irritated by your altar, it needs to change. When you do anything to your altar, it's a good idea to light a candle and some sage or incense and sit for a few minutes to center yourself before you start.

Change your altar from this centered place. Every few months I do a major altar cleaning. I remove everything from the altar and wash or dust it. I clean my crystals in salt water and sunlight or moonlight. Then I smudge everything that's going back on the altar with sage and lavender before replacing it.

Remember that this is your altar and that it is there for you. It should reflect your sense of what makes you feel happy, calm, and centered. You can change it whenever you want; the garden is a good analogy. You have a basic structure in your garden, but you still move plants around, plant new ones, and prune here and there. If you bear this in mind, your altar or altars will always feel full of life and energy, and will be a resource for you when you need to come to center.

And don't forget beauty. It's an important aspect of the altar. Your altar should please your eyes, calm your mind, and soothe your heart.

---

## WHAT TO DO THIS MONTH

This month, create your altar. If you don't have an altar yet, then enjoy the journey of creating your first one—a special focus in your home for your spiritual practice. If you already have an altar, spend some extra time sitting in front of it. See if you want to change it or if you want to create an additional altar in another part of your home.

Whether you are making an altar for the first time or replenishing an existing one, invoke the spirits of joy and play as well as those of dedication and prayer as you enter this creative task. Let yourself loose with this process and allow your intuition to lead you to the fabrics, colors, and artifacts that make you happy and will best nourish your spiritual practice now.

# Lesson 3

# PERSONAL HISTORY
# AND MOTIVATION

● ◐ ◑ ○ ○ ◑ ◐ ●

Just do it.
—NIKE ADVERTISING SLOGAN

The demands of daily life can seem to collide with our best intentions to maintain good habits of spiritual practice. Mindful attention to the duties of daily life is part of holistic spiritual practice, but this is nourished and made possible by taking time out to center, contemplate, and commune. Yet all too often we find ourselves overwhelmed and distracted by the mundane world.

Why do we procrastinate about spiritual practice? Why is it so often a struggle to make the time to sit quietly, to pray, and to meditate? You may really want to make an altar, get more centered, and contact your inner wisdom, yet you find yourself procrastinating about fully embracing these actions and practices. Many people find that their good intentions get swamped by the duties of daily life and their spiritual life never gets the attention it needs to flower. In this lesson, I'm going to explore ways to process this inner conflict and enable the shift into a more harmonious, smooth relationship with the spiritual realm.

Motivation in any self-generated endeavor can be hard to find. For most of us, some kind of a structure and some sense of belonging can help to keep us connected to our practice. But for many people today, there is no group, no church, no one place or entity that feels authentic and that fits into the rest of one's life. We have to learn to do it by ourselves.

## ORGANIZED RELIGION

It's pretty much a given that if you are reading this, you have found that organized religion doesn't completely fulfill your spiritual needs. Going to church one day a week gives people a useful structure, and it used to be a social requirement. It may be to our collective detriment that this is no longer so and that churchgoing has been replaced by trips to temples of retail. It is arguable that this social change would have taken a somewhat different route if the religions had truly served us and our needs in the present.

For example, going to church can be uplifting, but most services are only briefly contemplative. The experience can be rather like putting a toe into a huge ocean and pulling it straight out again as soon as you feel the water on your feet. Some religions are more contemplative in approach, such as Buddhism and the monastic traditions of Christianity, but these also demand self-motivation. It seems that if you want depth, want to really develop, want to achieve the kind of wise cen-teredness that you know intuitively is possible for human beings to achieve, and if you want a deep and continuous experience, you have to develop your own practice and stick to it.

## SPIRITUAL TEACHERS

Having a teacher can be enormously helpful, because ideally you then have someone to report back to—someone who is monitoring your progress, who has trodden the path before you, and whose wisdom you can incorporate through osmosis. But for many people, finding a spiritual teacher is a hard thing to do and requires a level of commit-ment that might not fit with the rest of one's life.

Too often, finding a teacher involves a cult-like immersion that understandably puts off a lot of people. Running off to India or joining an ashram could be destructive to other important commitments and elements of one's life. And then there are the scandals concerning spiritual teachers and abuse, whether sexual, financial, or emotional. I recommend great discrimination with spiritual teachers, especially if they claim to be enlightened.

A true teacher is not in it for the ego; does not abuse his or her students sexually, financially, emotionally, or behaviorally; and shows a consistent ability to offer spiritual illumination about life. Teachers who are genuinely wise and light-filled don't glamorize or mythologize their own spiritual development. Instead they are transparent about their own nature, and about both the joys and the difficulties of the path.

It takes time to see if your potential teacher measures up to these criteria. The Dalai Lama says you should observe a teacher for twelve years before making a commitment to him/her. That's a long time, but his advice is a good rule of thumb.

It's a wonderful blessing if you find a true teacher, but if you haven't met such a person or are still checking him or her out, it doesn't mean you can't develop by yourself. Being an independent spiritual practitioner means finding the inner teacher—that part of your own being that acts as an external spiritual teacher would by encouraging your practice and being a wise, kind inner voice.

Whether or not you find a genuine spiritual teacher to work with, there are always teachers in life. Sometimes they may not be incarnated, and sometimes they may be unexpected and not appear in an explicitly spiritual context. Life itself is a great and continuous teacher.

## SPIRITUAL PRACTICE AS A CREATIVE PATH

Creating your own spiritual practice is a creative act. The same rules to sustaining creative work pretty much apply here. You need to find the way that works for you, you need to find balance within the work, and you need to work through your psychological blocks to having that much fulfillment in life. All these factors work together, because how can you find the way that works for you unless you find the motivation to begin?

This motivation may begin out of a sense of desperation, longing, or even depression and a sense of something crucial being missing. The energy that is really behind this sense of longing, that really is pushing you past your usual comfort zone, and that will give you the strength to continue, is your deep-down love of life. When you contact your inner respect for the life force that flows through you, your connection with the spiritual realm will begin to feel solid. This is one of the reasons why being in nature connects us with spiritual truth and information, and why healthy living—taking good care of your body—is part of holistic spiritual development.

It could be said that it is your karma to have a soul that can recognize the spiritual dimension, yet at the same time it appears to be a freely chosen matter when you make the fundamental decision to honor the life force by living as full, passionate, and truthful a life as you can. (By *truthful* I mean being true to your soul purpose and life path, although I will add that simply telling the truth is a great spiritual practice. *The Four Agreements* by Don Miguel Ruiz has more information on this.)

## FINDING YOUR OWN PATH

First of all, relax. Spirituality is fundamentally straightforward, and at its core level, you know how to do it. Human beings have been doing this forever. Prayer and spiritual communion probably predate making fire in the human story. Awe, wonder, and the sense that there is more to all of this than meets the eye, are perennial in human experience.

Let yourself break the rules. Let yourself have fun with the journey. Let yourself be still for long enough to begin to really listen. Give yourself the gift of hours spent in nature doing nothing.

When you wake in the night for no reason, lie quietly and feel the darkness. Open yourself to your higher self, your spiritual guidance, and the wisdom that is all around you.

There is a technology of spiritual work, and it has been developed over many centuries and all over the world. Techniques for spiritual practice are just that—techniques. You can learn them, choosing the ones you like best and feel the most affinity with. You can adapt them and make them your own. If you don't like any mantras you find, make one up that pleases you. Someone originally made them up, and you can carry on this tradition of spiritual creativity. This is not to diminish the very real power of the ancient Sanskrit mantras, for example, but there's no point in chanting something if it doesn't feel right to you, especially when it comes from a tradition you weren't born into or raised in, and is in a language you don't understand. (There's much more in Lesson 5 on meditation and mantras.)

So far, the techniques I have talked about in this book have been fundamental ones shared across religions. Keep in mind that whether they are chanting or meditation or altar building, they are all largely methods for stilling the mind and opening your being to the spiritual realm. Honor the traditions, but don't be hidebound by them. Spiritual practice should be alive. It should be relevant. Otherwise your practice will soon feel stale, and you won't want to do it.

## CREATE BALANCE WITHIN THE WORK

To find the motivation to practice regularly, you need to find a way of practicing that brings you enough pleasure in the moment without being indulgent or trite. If it's too hard, you won't want to continue, and if it's too soft and mushy, you won't get anything out of it. Pulling a divination card each day, such as an Angel or a Tarot card, might help you focus on the issues at hand, but it won't help you to deepen and strengthen as a being, or at least not very effectively. Making yourself do sitting meditation for hours in an uncomfortable position, with your knees in agony, won't necessarily make you a better person, but it will mess up your knees. Stay alert and intent, but don't force or coerce yourself: it's counterproductive in the long run.

## PERSONAL HISTORY

I've left this for last because of, and not in spite of, the fact that it is so
crucial. It's where I recommend you do your work this month. I'm
going to give you an exercise to help you work through this territory.
Our background—our family, society, and education—has a powerful
influence on our spiritual development and can either aid or disturb it.

Sometimes childhood experiences around religion are so trau-
matic that they create psychological blocks and mean we come to
associate concepts of God or prayer with fear and danger. People educated in strict religious schools and/or raised in extremely religious
households may develop an aversion to religion because they associate
it with a punitive upbringing.

At the other end of the spectrum, one may have had a pseudo-
religious childhood in which spiritual life was only discussed in terms
that were cozy and sweet but lacked depth. In this kind of environment, the growing young person's experience doesn't mature through
initiation at adolescence into a more meaningful understanding of the
spiritual dimension of being. Memories and early training are too simple and saccharine to actually give anything of real use and meaning
for grappling with the moral and practical complexities of adult life.

Most Westerners get only an initiation of a material kind at the
onset of puberty—new clothes, a first bra, and so on—and later, a
fumbling sexual initiation bereft of any spiritual context. This lack of
spiritual initiation at adolescence means that religion becomes dry for
us. It fails to meet us where we need it, so we give up and life becomes
spiritually barren. Often, spiritually minded teens turn to drugs and
alcohol as a way of attaining the kind of ecstatic, transpersonal states
they crave, and to deal with the spiritual confusion they feel yet cannot articulate.

These are just some of the issues that can result in inner conflict later
in life, when you know that you want and need to have more spiritual
connection, but you find yourself unwilling to commit to a regular practice and to give yourself the gift of time spent in communion.

At this point, it's time to do some recapitulation in order to remember your spiritual history and think about how you got here.

## CHARTING YOUR PERSONAL SPIRITUAL HISTORY

Give yourself at least a good couple of hours to do this exercise. Sit somewhere pleasant and nurturing, maybe in front of your altar or out in nature, and let yourself dig deep into your memory banks.

Here are some questions to help stimulate your memory about your personal spiritual history. I suggest you write down the answers in a journal or notebook.

1.  What religion were you born into, if any?
2.  How do or did your parents relate to the spiritual realm? What did they inherit from their families? Are there any religiously related traumas in your bloodline, such as persecution, holocaust, pogroms, or exile? If there was no religious observance in your childhood, see if you can find out when and where the rupture occurred. When did you family stop identifying with and practicing a religion?
3.  Did your parents or grandparents pass on any spiritual habits to you, such as daily prayer or a seasonal ritual? Did they pass on a strong moral code or spiritual values?
4.  As a small child, do you remember being supported by your spiritual awareness? Did it help you cope with life? Did it involve your family? How did it manifest?
5.  Do you remember being troubled by religious or spiritual matters as a child? Were you taught to be afraid, for example, of the devil or of ghosts?
6.  If you went to religious services as a child, cast yourself back and remember what it felt like to you. What did it smell like? What did you like? What didn't you like? If you stopped or changed your religious attendance, when did you stop going and why?
7.  How did your education deal with religion and spirituality?

8.  How did your early religious training and experience influ-
    ence the way you felt about yourself? As a human being? As a
    boy or girl? At adolescence, did it have any influence on your
    ideas about sexuality or about your changing body?

9.  How did your childhood religious experience influence the
    way you thought of your future?

10. Was there a being in the religious pantheon of your childhood
    whom you related to personally, either as a role model or
    someone you could pray to or talk to?

11. When was the first time you remember having a personal spiri-
    tual experience—an insight into the numinous? Write down
    what happened in detail.

12. Recall other times when you felt close to the ineffable, when
    the meaning of life felt very near, when you felt in touch with
    something beyond the personal and the mundane.

13. Have you ever had a peak experience, a sense of being one
    with everything? How did it happen, and how has it influ-
    enced your life?

This is big territory in your personal and family history, so don't
be surprised if you find yourself resisting the work or feeling very
emotional at times as you progress through the questions. Use your
journal to express your feelings and to clarify your memories. If you
need to do some digging into your family's spiritual heritage, consider
asking older relatives for information.

●  ●  ◖  ○  ◐  ◗  ●

Finding a steady stream of motivation for spiritual practice develops
over time. Setting achievable goals is a good strategy for developing
depth and consistency in practice. You could, for example, make a commitment to yourself to sit every day for a month and do a certain prayer
or meditation, even if it is very simple and short. Then when the month
is up, think about what effect the practice had. How different do you

feel now? Was your mood noticeably calmer and happier during this month? Did your life speed up in terms of synchronicities and moving forward with other stuck patterns? Did you have any aha moments about emotional processes in your life? Make notes in your journal of whatever comes up at this time, and then make a new commitment for your next phase.

Remember that we take periodic breaks from everything we do in life, even eating. Allowing such breaks is part of healthy spirituality. It doesn't help to be too fixated on regularity; we first need to clear the weeds in the garden. That means understanding where our spiritual history might be obstructing our development now. So do the exercise on your personal history before you move on to the next topic: clearing the mind.

---

## WHAT TO DO THIS MONTH

If you don't already have a journal, buy one to do this month's exercise. Then for the future, make notes on your experiences during the course of these lessons, and write down your dreams and other insights that come to you over this coming year. Beginning to take your spiritual practice more seriously or being more diligent about it will bring up a lot of information. It's good to have a place to keep it all written down so you can refer back to it.

If you have the time and energy, it's a good idea to personalize your journal. Stick a picture on the cover or make a collage on it. You can use images that inspire you and reflect the issues you are dealing with at the current time.

Now that you've created your altar and sacred space, try to find time on a regular basis to sit in front of the altar. If you already have a practice such as meditation or chanting, do it. If not, just sit for now and relax.

You can do Tarot readings, write in your journal, or do yoga—all in front of your altar. It's your space for *you*, for getting to know yourself and your deepest dreams, for nourishing yourself, and for communing with your guidance.

If you haven't already done so, establish a daily habit of lighting a candle and some incense or smudge, and playing sacred sounds in your room. If you already do this, keep it up.

Keep your eyes out for whatever you still need for your altar, and every now and then buy or pick some fresh flowers for it. Remember that the altar is an outer manifestation of your spiritual life, and reflects back to you your devotion to your inner spiritual garden. This care and attention to your altar helps to sustain your motivation and anchor your practice.

# Lesson 4

# CLEARING THE MIND AND GROUNDING THE BODY

● ◐ ◑ ○ ◔ ◐ ●

*The secret of health for both mind and body is not to mourn for the*
*past, not to worry about the future, not to anticipate troubles,*
*but to live the present moment wisely and earnestly.*
—THE BUDDHA

*The body is a sacred garment. It's your first and last garment;*
*it is what you enter life in and what you depart life with,*
*and it should be treated with honor.*
—MARTHA GRAHAM

You've cleared your space, set up your altar, and addressed your personal history and motivational issues. The next step is to develop techniques to clear the mind, and fully inhabit and ground the body. The mind and body work together; they are not as separate as we might think. But how they interface is not totally straightforward. We can be physically ill and have great insights; we can be physically well and be insensitive to our own needs as well as those of others.

The dreaming spirit behind life expresses itself through the wholeness of our being, using the mind and the body. Both clarity of mind and grounded, activated embodiment are integral to spiritual development. As we awaken spiritually and develop inner clarity, our experience of our corporeality changes: subtle energies develop and flow, and we became aware of a streaming of energy—a sense of aliveness in our cells. Some traditions have developed specific exercise regimes, such as t'ai chi and yoga, that are designed to both strengthen the body and clarify the mind. During meditation, as the mind calms and clears, the body relaxes and energy flows. And it works the other way around, too: when we exercise and spend time in nature, the mind gets calmer.

43

## CLEARING THE MIND

When the mind is full of concepts, worries, fears, and controlling agendas, we lack mental clarity. When our thoughts and reactions arise out of such a cluttered state, we don't have access to our full awareness; we are half asleep and stumbling through life.

When we can pay full attention purely in the present, at will, then we are truly free. This is the key to liberation. It is not that the past and future are irrelevant, but when we are run by leftover emotions and past attachments, or anxieties and desires about the future—especially when they are only subliminally conscious—we don't have all our energy and attention available for the present moment.

Once we learn to let go of the attachments that do not exist in present time or cannot be fulfilled in present time, all the psychic energy previously caught up in longing and feeling is available to us. Then, paradoxically, it becomes much more likely that we will achieve what we truly desire. We have the opportunity to really hear within what we truly want, and we have the energy to move forward and take the necessary steps to enable it to happen.

Clearing the mind allows deep knowing to flower and to be heard. This is one of the primary purposes of meditation. That deep knowing tells us what it is we really want and how to get there. It usually gives us information about an action a step at a time, although there are times when a long stream of steps will be laid out in front of us, especially when we have to make a big leap. This helps us, psychologically, to instigate deep changes.

We also need to protect the mind from too much worry and distress by managing our lives skillfully to minimize unnecessary stress. We also protect the mind by being careful about how much difficult information we expose ourselves to. Images of violence and abuse can injure the mind. Don't be asleep to the suffering of the world, but don't overburden yourself either.

Here are some preliminary steps that help support the process of mental clearing.

## THE MIND

The word *mind* is another way of saying "awareness." There isn't any literal, physical mind. Yes, consciousness is strongly related to brain activity, but it is not only that; it is something that appears to be both personal and transpersonal, and that is constantly being fed and influenced by your physical body and your surroundings and experiences.

Consciousness exists in the entire physical body, not only in the brain. The whole body has memories and information within its cells, and there are connections from all parts of the body via the chakras to the other energy bodies, all of which feed into and influence each other. Names for the other energy bodies include the soul, the emotional body, and the etheric body. There are various ways of describing these energy bodies in various traditions, but rather than go into them here, I would rather you open yourself to your own experience and see what is real for you.

The deep knowing that arises in a clear mind is also known as spiritual guidance. Just exactly where personal consciousness stops and the higher self—or even God—begins is another interesting matter for personal inquiry.

## MENTAL CLUTTER

Clear awareness allows for openness to inner truth and deep knowing. To experience clarity of awareness we need to get rid of our mental clutter.

What do I mean by mental clutter? Think of it this way: in your home, when you don't keep up with the dishes and the garbage, the place becomes messy and smelly. It's hard to cook in the kitchen because it's full of stuff, and you can't find things because the house is so messy. Life becomes less than optimally functional.

It's the same with your mind. If you don't stay current with your emotional life, with your thoughts and feelings, your awareness becomes cluttered with all the unacknowledged experiences and information. And when you don't stay current with your activities in your outer life, your awareness becomes cluttered with thoughts about all the things you should have done and should be doing.

Think of the following suggestions as feng shui for the mind.

## WAYS TO CLEAR MENTAL CLUTTER

1.  **Keep a Journal**
    Keeping a journal is a very effective way of developing self-knowledge and clearing mental clutter. As discussed in the last chapter, I highly recommend that you buy a journal and develop a habit of taking fifteen minutes every day (at least) to write down how you are feeling and the significant things that have happened, and to record your dreams and any synchronicities or hints that came to you during the day. Once you have written something down, you have given yourself a chance to express the accompanying feelings, and you have more detachment and more room in your mind.

2.  **Talk It Over**
    You can also clear your thoughts and express your feelings through talking with another person. Make sure you talk to someone you can trust—someone who won't make you feel worse, won't amplify any tendency to excess self-pity or playing the victim when you aren't really, or won't prescribe actions before you've had a chance to work things out for yourself. For these reasons, a good therapist or counselor can be very useful, especially during times of so much activity and turmoil that you can't keep up with yourself.

3.  **Express Your Emotions**
    Both writing and talking help activate your emotional expression. The next step is to allow direct expression of those emotions. If you're sad or overwhelmed and you feel like crying, let yourself cry. Weeping is one of the single most

transformative things we can do, and it unleashes a cascade of physiological responses in the body that are directly related to clearing the mind. It greatly accelerates our ability to process thoughts and move forward. If you feel angry, beat on a pillow. I know this might sound silly, but it really does work. We are physical creatures, and making an accompanying movement to match our feelings helps release stuck energy and thoughts, thus clearing the mind.

4.  **Get Over Procrastination: Work with Edges**
    In process-oriented psychology, "the edge" is the term used to describe the territory in between the known and the unknown, the past and the future, and our current concept of ourselves and what we subconsciously want to become. We often stall at the point of action because the unknown is on the other side of that action.

    We get caught at the edge and hold ourselves back. This is one of the prime ways we accumulate mental clutter and hold back our natural developmental path. The concept of the edge describes how fear, insecurity, lack of self-belief, laziness, and over-attachment to convention can paralyze processes of self-development that are innate and natural.

    Human beings are naturally spiritual, and this spirituality is not separate from daily life. But we live in a time when much that is natural in us has been controlled to the point that we have to work quite hard to reconnect with natural impulses.

    If you find yourself unable to do something you have planned to do such as meditate regularly, you may well be stuck at an edge. And more mundane actions you are stalling on can also block your spiritual practice by clogging your mind and generating anxiety.

    To begin to deal with this, make a list of things you are procrastinating on. Then make a realistic plan of action. If for some reason it is not yet time for the action in question, then accept this: sometimes we waste energy and sabotage ourselves by pushing too hard on something that just isn't ripe for action. But if you know you are lagging behind with something you really should just get on with, inquire within (for example, by using your journal) as to why.

Make a list of these tasks, and then write down what you can do about them and when. Note if anything seems too daunting and think about whom you can ask to help you with it. We sometimes get stuck with our processes these days because we live in a very individualistic society, but we aren't necessarily designed to do everything on our own. Sometimes we need help. You don't have to do everything by yourself. Many tasks are too difficult to do alone, and if you can find a way to share them with someone else, they suddenly become doable.

See if you can do a trade with a friend. If you have to make a phone call that is scary or intimidating, or fill out some paperwork you don't understand, ask someone to do it for you, and then do something for him or her in return. If you have taken on too many commitments and are overwhelmed by your responsibilities, ask for help.

It's not written anywhere that you have to do everything in your life yourself. Sharing the load can make everything work much better. And sometimes just accepting this and allowing someone to help makes it easier to do it yourself the next time around, or to plan more realistically so that you don't have more than you can handle on your plate.

## 5.  Examine Your Beliefs

Our beliefs are wrapped up in a big messy bundle with procrastination over actions and the failure to complete unacknowledged emotional processes. Ask yourself which beliefs are engaging in the process. Do you feel hopeless? Do you fear who you will be on the other side of the action? Do you feel capable of sorting out your problems?

Asking these questions may take you into such a deep inquiry that you enter the territory of the Big Beliefs, where you ask questions such as: Do you believe your life has a meaning? Do you believe in a superior spiritual power? What do you believe about life in general? These questions of existence are huge topics and can take a whole lifetime to explore. For now, try to stick to examining the beliefs that most obviously and directly have an impact on your capacity to stay current with yourself.

6. **Let Go of Worries and Anxieties**
Make a list of everything you are worried about, then put it away for a day. Come back and take a hard look at it. Are any of these worries based in reality? If they are, take any action you need to take. Make a list of what you will do. Then burn the first piece of paper with all the worries on it, and promise yourself to let go of bad worry habits and of thinking the worst.

A very useful way of looking at worries is to see them as prayers in reverse. Worries are an internalization of our lack of faith. If you turn the worry around and make it into a prayer, you will often find that the answer comes to you from your inner voice, a dream, a synchronicity, or from someone else.

## EMBODIMENT

The body gives us information all the time; we just have to learn to listen to it. Body awareness is an integral part of spiritual development. If we don't pay attention to the body, we become unbalanced, accident-prone, and unwell. Doing a lot of spiritual practice without factoring in the body can worsen this imbalance.

Staying fit and healthy will keep your body strong and help keep your mind clear. In this way, you will avoid the trap of becoming too

airy-fairy and spaced-out, which can afflict people who focus on the
spiritual aspect of living.

The minimum we need to do is eat nutritious food at regular inter-
vals and walk daily in fresh air. If it suits you, it's also good to find the
time to work out at the gym and to swim in pools or lakes.

The influence of Asian religions in past decades has brought an
influx of physical exercises, such as yoga and t'ai chi, that are considered part and parcel of focused spiritual development within their
traditions. If you haven't investigated these methods already, look
around your area for teachers and classes, and try out a few. See what
works best for you.

## THE BELLY

The focal point of many of these forms of exercise is the belly, known
as the *hara* in Japan and as the *tan-tien* in China. This is not simply the
place where you digest your food, but also the body's center of gravity
and the place where we experience and generate our core strength. A
weak *hara* makes it difficult for us to navigate our way through life,
make good decisions, and keep a clear head when engaging with spiritual material.

To feel into your *hara*, place the palm of your hand immediately
below your navel and focus on that area. See if you can feel a place of
concentrated energy a few inches below the navel and about a centime-
ter or so inside the belly. You should feel a sensation of slight buzzing or
heat, or at least a subtle difference from the area immediately around it.
The actual distance the *hara* falls below the navel varies, depending on
your height, weight, and gender. It falls a little lower in women than in
men because women usually have a lower center of gravity due to the
difference in body shape.

When you have located the *hara*, breathe into it gently, allowing
your energy there to fill up like a chalice filled to overflowing with a
warm, strong light.

These days the cultural focus on what constitutes desirable body
shape means that both men and women are often concerned about hav-

ing a noticeable belly, developing a corresponding tendency to tighten that area of the body. Good stomach muscles are a great thing to develop as long as we exercise them properly and don't create more tension in that area. If you are worried about having a belly, don't inhibit your core energy at the *hara* by breathing shallowly and contracting those muscles in an attempt to pull your stomach in. Ideally the belly should be both strong and relaxed, and fully inhabited by your awareness.

## GROUNDING EXERCISES

If you find yourself feeling nervous, stressed out, and agitated, you can very quickly ground yourself and release the anxiety by connecting to the earth energetically. It's a good idea to develop a habit of grounding so that you have more resilience and your spiritual practice always stays rooted in common sense.

Here is a series of short exercises to ground you. First, start with the feet.

### FEET ON THE EARTH

If you can, do this outside in bare feet on the earth. If that's not practical, you can do it perfectly well inside. However you do this exercise, make sure your feet are warm.

Standing in a relaxed pose, knees shoulder-width apart and very slightly bent, with your arms hanging loosely at your sides, sink all your attention down to the soles of your feet, and feel them and how they contact the earth.

Roll out the outside of each foot slightly so it fully touches the ground. Stretch your toes and lift them slightly. Then bring them down to fully contact the earth. Roll your foot in slightly so the instep touches the earth. Press back on your heels. Then rest your whole foot gently on the earth, and breathe in and out a few times.

Now inhale fully. As you exhale, release the whole of each foot into the earth, feeling each part of the foot and each toe fully contacting and releasing into the earth. Feel how they rest peacefully in a full and trusting relationship with the ground. Now begin to walk very slowly, feeling with each step how each foot meets the earth sweetly and fully. Walk around a little and then stop for the next part.

## YOUR ENERGY TAIL

With your feet firmly contacting the ground, loosen your knees by letting them waggle a bit, and fully stretch out your hands, arms, shoulders, and spine for a count of ten. Then come back to simple standing, with your feet shoulders-width apart, arms hanging loosely by your sides. Breathe in deeply. As you breathe out, let your energy settle into your pelvis and feet.

Now imagine a tail of energy that originates deep in your pelvis and flows down out of your coccyx (tail bone) and down the back of your legs, past the back of your heels and deep into the earth. This tail gently keeps you rooted as you go about your daily activities. It pulls your head and shoulders back slightly so that you stand upright and don't go through life at a forward tilt. Visualizing this tail helps keep you in touch with your innate common sense.

## BUBBLING SPRING

At the same time that your grounding root flows down into the earth, energy comes up from the earth and into the point on the soles of your feet, just below your big and second toes. The Chinese call this area under the foot "Bubbling Spring," and understand it as the place where we receive pure energy from the earth. Let this part of your foot contact the earth as you walk, and imagine a stream of clear, fresh, rejuvenating energy flowing up into the sole of your foot. Then see it going up the insides of your legs and into your torso, particularly into your lower back and kidneys.

## BREATHING INTO THE BELLY

As you gently walk around your garden or room with your feet meeting the ground without equivocation, tail softly connecting you deep into the earth and Bubbling Spring Point activated to receive energy, now feel your belly. Feel if it is tight, contracted, or tense anywhere. Breathe deeply into your lower belly, allowing it to fully inflate and then releasing it as you exhale. With or without the walking, this is an instant way to relax, and it helps strengthen your core awareness.

If you like, you can keep walking slowly and mindfully, using these exercises as the basis for a walking meditation.

## SOCIAL ACTIVISM AND LOOKING OUTWARD

A parallel step to these inner-focused methods of physical and mental healing is to focus outward, onto other people. Helping others is a great way of calming the mind and grounding the body, and it allows for a healthier perspective. Helping others gives us a real experience of our connectedness in the web of life, and it is a crucial part of the spiritual journey.

It's true that some people are genuine, full-time contemplatives and hermits. But even hermits (for example, the Buddhist nun Tenzin Palmo) usually have to emerge at some point to give to others.

Even if you feel far from having a great mission in life and simply feel confused and lacking in clarity, you will find that reaching out and giving some of your time and attention can be balancing for you.

It is an error to think that you need to be fully sorted out before you can help others. The important thing is not to overstretch but to do something within your capacity that utilizes your natural strengths and that you enjoy. If you are not currently engaged in some activity that draws you into a helpful and generous relationship with society, keep an eye out for opportunities. Even doing something apparently very small will shift your perspective.

―――――――――――― ∞∞ ――――――――――――

## WHAT TO DO THIS MONTH

This chapter is pretty dense, and it's a lot of work to do each of the exercises properly. I suggest you do as many of the activities as you can, and come back later to any sections you don't have time for now. All the tools in this chapter are very useful methods to have in your personal awareness tool kit.

At the same time, look out this month for new opportunities to engage with the world around you.

# Lesson 5

# MEDITATION, PRAYER, AND SPIRITUAL GUIDANCE

● ◐ ◑ ○ ◑ ◑ ●

That meditator becomes eternally free who is able to withdraw
from external phenomena by fixing his gaze within the mid-spot
of the eyebrows; and to control his sensory mind and his intellect;
to free himself from desire, fear and anger.
— BHAGAVAD GITA

To pray is an act of power because it is an agreement between
the human and the divine, and we invest our faith in that agreement.
— DON MIGUEL RUIZ, *Prayers: A Communion with Our Creator*

In this month's lesson, we're going to look into meditation and
prayer, and the related subject of who we pray to and/or meditate
on. We'll explore the theme of our spiritual guidance and our connection with the divine, and look at how we can tap into that connection
so that it becomes as familiar to us as our family members, pets, and
closest friends. While we will still feel awe at the spiritual dimensions
of life, we can also feel at home; we can experience sustenance, nurturing, and relaxation within our spiritual communion.

## MEDITATION

We can work on having a clear and peaceful mind in two ways: directly
(as in the exercises in the previous chapter) or indirectly. Indirect methods are manifold. They include taking a vacation, watching TV, sleeping
and dreaming, doing something fun, doing something helpful for others,
doing something dangerous, and changing your state of consciousness
through rituals, medicines/drugs, or sex. We all have our preferred
ways to balance our mental state, to soothe anxiety and to calm down.

Some of these methods are more useful than others, some are easier to achieve than others, and some are safer than others. All can be done at different levels of consciousness, rendering the results more or less valuable, on a scale that varies from very effective to causing more problems in the long run.

Meditation is a time-honored and effective method that is both direct and indirect. In meditating, you have a clear intention to calm the mind, empty the mind, and still the mind. At the same time, meditation has an indirect effect on your worries and concerns by changing your brain chemistry and altering your consciousness so that you naturally relax and gain a different perspective. In time, you become a less mentally cluttered, less anxious, more capable, and more peaceful person.

In a sense, we can say that any attempt to relax the body and calm the mind is a meditation. But the concept of meditation has a more purposeful and spiritual connotation than most of the other activities we engage in to clear the mind.

The word *meditation* actually means to think about something deeply; the act of meditating, contemplation, reflection, and the contemplation of spiritual matters, especially as a religious practice.

When I first began investigating meditation in my twenties, I had a hard time with it. I could find a sense of inner peace when I meditated in a large group, but by myself I was hopeless. I found the concept of meditation overwhelming, and I think that feeling really got in the way. I was an overly self-conscious meditator. I thought it sounded rather grand and special to say, "I'm going to meditate now," and in the milieu I lived in then, it was indeed unusual.

I wasn't close to anyone who meditated regularly, so I didn't have a sense of it as an ordinary, daily thing to do. I thought that only very focused, organized, really spiritual people would meditate regularly, and that wasn't me. I had spiritual ambitions, but I had a hard time relating to being that focused. It was enough for me to organize my domestic life and my work. Organizing a meditation practice on top of that seemed like overkill. But I was definitely intrigued, and I felt enough of a hole in my center and a nagging sense of disconnection from both myself and from something unnameable that I knew I needed to take action.

I began to force myself out of bed at 7 AM to sit in front of my altar and stare at a candle, trying not to think. I would try really hard to have an empty, peaceful mind. Predictably, this didn't work, and I would feel as edgy and annoyed at the end of the requisite half hour as I had at the beginning, when I had pried myself out of a warm bed. I kept up this mental and physical torture for many months before I gave up, convinced that meditation was not for me and wondering what all the fuss was about.

But I noted the disparity of my private experience with the good experiences I had at a Buddhist center, in a group of other meditators. There I had entirely new experiences, such as finding myself in a waking dream, staring out over a vast lake that filled me with a deep sense of peace. I had no way of explaining this other than that it appeared to be connected to the mind-pool of the meditators.

Time went on, and I continued to study Buddhism when I could. I gradually began to gain a sense of self-confidence and felt less daunted by the concept of meditation and contemplative spiritual practice. At the same time, I embarked on a period of shamanic study that entailed periods of isolation and various initiations that had a cumulative effect upon my awareness. Most of this study was spent in nature and was very healing.

I didn't go back to forcing myself to meditate. At that stage, it clearly wasn't a workable tactic. But what I found over time was that if I just sat still, not doing anything, especially if I could sit outside in a peaceful, natural environment, meditation would naturally occur. That is, my mind would empty of nonessentials, and I would find myself contemplating whatever really mattered to me at the time and finding answers. So clarity of mind began.

Later, I studied meditation in more depth and found ways to meditate that worked for me, and I share some of these here.

## BEGINNING TO MEDITATE

The natural state of the mind, unobscured by thoughts and concerns, is like a clear sky, vast and open. To access this state we need to cultivate a relaxed and unforced attitude to meditation. Because the unobscured mind is part of nature, and is like the sky, it helps to meditate outdoors, preferably with a big view. The following very simple practice is a great way to begin to meditate.

Of course, there are many times when the weather, or our schedule, or the place we live, means that going outside is not practical. If this is the case, imagining your mind as a big, open, clear sky is very helpful. You can still follow the steps outlined below, but imagine the natural world instead of experiencing it directly.

Every day, or as often as possible, go alone to a place of natural beauty—your backyard or garden, a hillside, or the beach, if you are lucky enough to live near one. If the sun is shining or the moon is out, and if you can find a place near water of some kind, all the better.

- Sit on the ground or on a rock and get as comfortable as you can. There is no need to strain your body in any way when meditating.
- Sit with your back straight and your legs crossed, if you can. Place your hands softly on your knees.
- Keep your eyes gently open.
- Breathe.
- With gentle eyes, notice what you see.
- Feel the breath of the wind on your face.
- Settle into your sitting place.
- Let your breath sink down into your belly. Breathe deeply.
- Let your breath expand your heart and throat. Breathe deeply.
- Let your breath go down to the base of your spine. Breathe deeply.

- Let your breath go up to the crown of your head. Breathe deeply.
- Let your breath go down into the earth beneath you. Breathe deeply.
- Let your breath go up into the sky above you. Breathe deeply.
- Feel the gentle expansion of your energy field upward, downward, and outward, connecting with all things.
- Now bring your attention gently back to the belly.
- Breathe steadily, normally, and happily into your belly.
- Sit in quiet contemplation of the beauty of life. Let go into this air, this earth, this sun, and this water.
- Sit for as long as you like.
- When you feel ready, get up and stretch. Breathe deeply.
- Move on with your day, taking the slow and centered rhythm from your meditation with you.

## PRAYER

Prayer and meditation are closely related. Prayer is our meeting place with the divine: it can give us a sense of union; it can be respectful and honoring; it can be supplicating—a request for what we need in life; it can be an expression of gratitude.

Meditation can be contemplative and stilling. It can also be a request through the incantation of repetitive prayer or mantra directed at a particular deity. Just as prayer honors the divine, mantras contain within them recognition of the greatness of a deity, or archetypal energy and syllables that connote respect.

The line between communion/contemplation and supplication/request is impossible to delineate. Even people who think they are beyond asking for anything and who insist they merely want to dwell in the perfection of the present moment still have human needs. Who is to say which unconscious forces shape the desire to connect with the divine, within or without? In times of great need, even those who consider themselves agnostic or atheist find themselves praying for assistance.

One thing is clear: quieting the mind through prayer and/or meditation and opening one's being to spiritual guidance facilitates a different state of consciousness in which wisdom (and/or clarity) becomes more accessible.

## METHODS OF PRAYER

There are two main ways to pray: following a prayer written by some-one else or making up your own. Actually, there are three, because you can also pray in a conversational style. Arnold Mindell calls this "having it out with God," and I have found it a very effective tech-nique for moving things along when life feels horribly stuck.

I remember once, after several months of struggling to make my living in Los Angeles and feeling tremendously frustrated, yelling at the top of my lungs (while standing by the ocean so I did-n't disturb anyone) to my then rather vague and undefined sense of the divine, "Send me a job!" The next day the phone rang, and I was hired for a good television job that I had interviewed for sev-eral months before.

A calmer version of having it out with God is when you just sit calmly and quietly, ask a question, and wait for the answer to float into your mind. I do this regularly. About once a month, usually at the new moon, I sit down with a pen and a piece of paper and ask, "What do I need to know?" and "What do I need to do?" Now, of course, whether or not the answers come from within or without is an unan-swerable question, but it leads us to the topic of spiritual guidance, which I'll get to in a moment.

Prayers of supplication work best when balanced with prayers of gratitude and a recognition of blessings. Whether or not the deities care about our gratitude, it certainly does us good to express it and to acknowledge our blessings. (There is a deeper investigation of grati-tude in Lesson 10.)

## TO WHOM DO WE PRAY?

Whom we pray to is a matter of individual taste and inclination, and the best way to explore this is to follow what you love. Which deities are you attracted to? Which ones make you laugh, make you feel peaceful, make you feel protected? Don't analyze this too much or second-guess yourself. If you like to have pictures of Jesus around, then do so. If the Dalai Lama is someone you find inspiring, have a picture of him on a wall or on your altar.

Displaying a picture of particular saints or spiritual teachers doesn't mean you have to belong to their religion (assuming they belong to one). It just means you recognize their particular style of spiritual belief and practice, and that it connects you to something that feels positive, helpful, and wise. Looking around as I write, I see that I have pictures of several teachers and spiritual beings above my desk. They've been put up on the wall over time (along with pictures of flowers and trees, and postcards of paintings by friends and by old masters), and each of them makes me feel happy, connecting me to my own wisdom.

There's a postcard of a beaming Don Miguel Ruiz (the author of *The Four Agreements*, and a wonderful spiritual teacher and shaman). This card is a potent image for me because I've had the good fortune to spend time with Don Miguel, and I well recall the warmth of his hugs, and the enormously supportive and loving resonance of his being.

I have a postcard of the Black Madonna of Einsiedeln in Switzerland carrying a little black baby Jesus. Next to her is a painting of Machig Labdrön, an eleventh-century yogini from Tibet, and a photograph of Lama Tsultrim Allione, a contemporary woman Buddhist teacher who I have also had the great good fortune to study with. These female figures connect me into the resonance of the actualized feminine by supporting my work and helping me connect to my strength as a woman.

And then I have a photograph of Carl Jung taken in his eighties, in which he emanates a slightly distant yet humorous kindness and a great intelligence. It's no accident that these are the people whose images I have placed above my desk over time, as they each represent facets of the wisdom traditions I have studied and that I draw on every day in my work.

Behind me on the mantelpiece sit the Dalai Lama, Tara, Vajrayogini, Shiva, and an Edward Burne-Jones version of Melchizedek (who looks exactly how my child self thought God looked: avuncular and friendly, with a big white beard, a crown, a halo, and a golden goblet). As you can see, I have no problem with mixing spiritual traditions, and having these pictures of wise, archetypal beings around makes it feel like home to me.

Sometime in the 1980s I realized that my upbringing had only offered male divine beings—God and Jesus—as models of spiritual perfection. In the church I was raised in, the Madonna was relegated to a side chapel; after all, she was "just" the mother and most definitely human. I came to understand that, as a woman, it was hard to access the divine within when one's outer images were all masculine. I began to look for images of the divine feminine, which led to a breakthrough in my level of spiritual comfort, and a growing sense of having open and unfettered access to my own spirituality.

The next step from having images of spiritual beings around you is to communicate with them purposefully, such as pray. This practice exists in all traditions, and while in general we think that talking to imaginary people is a sign of an unfit mind, when it comes to spiritual practice, all cultures suspend this notion and think that talking to a deity is quite normal (or at least not something that gets you carted off to the hospital).

## PRAYER BEADS AND MALAS

Prayer beads, rosaries, and malas are used in many religions and cultures to facilitate prayer and soothe the spirit. The action of moving the beads, touching each one, and repeating the circle over and over is calming. And each time you get to the end/beginning of the rosary or mala (a cross on a rosary and a larger bead known as the guru bead on a mala), you know you have completed one cycle of prayer or mantra recitation.

Different traditions favor different numbers of beads. The classic Buddhist mala is 108 beads long (one can also use divisions of that number, 54 or 27). Muslim prayer beads number 99 or 100. Catholic rosaries vary in length, depending on how many prayers are to be said. Some Christians use a 33-bead string—a chaplet—which corresponds to the 33 years of Christ's life on Earth.

A mala becomes very personal and full of your spiritual juju from the many times you touch it as you pray. In the Buddhist tradition, it is said that if a mala breaks, it does so to save you from a negative karmic event. Your mala is seen as an extension of your being, and therefore it can take some of your karma off your shoulders. Once I had an illness that was dramatically cured after my mala broke. I was really weak with anemia. Then my mala broke, and I rapidly recovered, with no treatment. At the time, I didn't know the belief about the mala helping you karmically, so I wasn't healed by suggestion. In fact, I thought that perhaps I had done something wrong for my mala to have broken.

What kind of mala you use is really a matter of personal preference. Malas are usually made from seeds, wood, bone, or semiprecious stones. If you want to be sure that you are using the right kind of mala for you, a Vedic (Indian) astrologer can look at your birth chart to determine the most effective material for your mala.

## MANTRAS

Mantras are short phrases that can be said either inside your own head or out loud as a whisper or chant. There are many, many mantras in the world, but you can make up your own to resonate with your preferred spiritual traditions. You can also make up mantras that can also be very effective. "I Love All" is a mantra, as is "I love life and life loves me" and "I am One with the Universe." You can also make up mantras that fit your current situation, like an affirmation such as "I have the courage I need."

To discover more or to learn more about mantras you already know, I recommend Andrew Harvey's book *The Direct Path* for its thorough explanations of some of the key prayers and mantras from different traditions.

There are some powerful ancient mantras in Sanskrit that are passed down to us in the Buddhist tradition. The syllables themselves have a mysterious power on one's body and energy field, and they work to calm the mind and firm up the connection with the spiritual realm. Here are two mantras I enjoy very much, find very beneficial, and chant often.

## OM MANI PADNE HUM

*Om Mani Padme Hum* (usually pronounced "Ohmmm MAH-Nee PAHD-May Hung") means "All hail to the jewel at the heart of the lotus." This means all hail to the joyous perfection of the heart that resides within each one of us and within the core of all life. This is the great mantra of Avalokitesvara (known as Chenrezig in Tibetan), the Buddhist deity of compassion. It is a widely known chant and is often inscribed on Indian and Tibetan jewelry and artifacts.

*Om Mani Padme Hum* is a powerful mantra for opening the heart. It softens the being and connects you into your own inner perfection, the place in you where perfect, unobstructed compassion and acceptance reside. It is also centering in that it pulls energy down from the head and into the heart, so it is a useful mantra when you have done a lot of intense crown chakra opening practice and feel unbalanced by too much spiritual work. You do not have to receive a transmission from a teacher to use this mantra or any of the other mantras recommended in this book; they are open to all.

## THE TARA MANTRA

The Tara mantra is *Om Tare Tutare Ture So Ha*, pronounced "Ohmmm Tah-ray Tuw-tar-ay Tuw-ray So-ha HAA" (extend the first and last syllables).

If you prefer the Indian version, you can say *Sva Ha* at the end instead of *So Ha*. Either version is a traditional mantra ending meaning "I bow to you."

Tara, the goddess of protection and compassion, is the primary female deity in the Tibetan Buddhist pantheon and one of the most worshipped deities in Tibet. She is saluted in this mantra as the noble, exalted liberator, the swift and glorious liberator, and the deity who grants success by removing obstacles and fulfilling all good intentions. In some ways similar to the Virgin Mary in the Catholic tradition, Tara listens to prayers, wants to help human beings, and represents miraculous action. Tara has many manifestations, most notably as Green Tara, goddess of the Earth who overcomes obstacles and saves people from danger, and as White Tara, guardian and deliverer of peace, longevity, and protection.

The Tara mantra is one of the most widely used mantras in Tibetan Buddhism. It works to liberate one of all fears, remove obstacles, and facilitate good intentions for the world. I have found it extremely powerful in my own life. In addition, the mantra is said to help with the well-being of the world in general. In these current times, reciting this mantra is a very useful practice, as it serves to calm one's own fears and, at the same time, emit a strong, positive intention.

If you get the chance to receive the Tara empowerment from a Tibetan teacher who has been empowered to make the transmission through a lineage, please take it. It will strengthen your practice.

You can sit and say the Tara mantra with a mala, one mantra for every bead. Go around the mala four times or however many times feels right to you. Or you can just say it in your head as you go about your day. The former method helps you focus and can be very useful when you have a particular problem. The solution will just come into your head after a while. The constant practice as one goes about one's daily life has a wonderful effect of stilling the mind, opening the heart, and concentrating one's actions into the most effective and most authentic avenues for one's own nature.

## YOUR OWN RELATIONSHIP
## WITH SPIRITUAL GUIDANCE

Your relationship with spiritual guidance is a very personal matter. To discover more about it, here is a writing exercise that will help you flesh out your knowledge of your own path.

Write a short piece on your experiences of spiritual guidance and where you feel that guidance came from.

1. Think of a period in your life when you were aware of receiving spiritual guidance. If it's hard for you to think of an example, think of a time you had a strong intuition about something and followed it, and it turned out to be very helpful or maybe even saved a life—yours or someone else's. Or, less dramatically, perhaps following that voice got you to do something that then generated a cascade of events that had an important effect on your life.
2. No matter whether it was apparently dramatic or not, describe at least one specific experience in which you felt spiritually guided.
3. Did this guidance feel like it came from within you or from some other source? Or do you have a sense of both being true?
4. If you have a sense of an outer source of guidance, does it have an identity, such as a spirit guide or a deity?

## HAPPINESS AND THE SPIRITUAL PATH

Inner joy, a kind of subtly bubbling inner sensibility, is an indicator of a spiritual path that suits you and is working well. The bottom line with any long-term spiritual practice is that it should engender an inner sense of peace and happiness, not necessarily all of the time but as an underlying sense of well-being. If it doesn't, then something is wrong.

Just because people do a lot of spiritual practice doesn't mean they are happy or peaceful. I have visited plenty of monasteries and spiritual communities where uptight and grumpy people were suppressing not just their instinctual needs but also their emotions and creativity.

This is not to say that doing regular spiritual practice means you won't have times of sadness or even of certain kinds of depression, because life will always periodically present us with challenges and with loss. However, a spiritual practice that works should operate as a resource that gives you fairly consistent access to the floor of joy that underpins all living things.

The mantras I gave you earlier in this chapter are particularly good for connecting you with the heart, with love, and with joy, as are many other mantras and prayers.

## WHAT TO DO THIS MONTH

For this month, instigate a regular daily practice of meditation and/or prayer. See if you can inculcate the habit (if you don't already have it) so that it becomes something that is automatically programmed into your day. If you don't like to sit still on a cushion, you don't have to. You can meditate while walking, lying in the bath, or sitting in the garden. Sitting cross-legged on the floor on a cushion has the advantage of keeping your back straight and your body still, which enhances the flow of energy and stillness of the mind, but it is not the only method. Experiment with what works best for you, and then continue that practice.

# Lesson 6

# DREAMS AND DEVELOPING THE IMAGINATION

● ● ◐ ○ ○ ◑ ◑ ●

Dreams are letters from the soul.
—CONNIE KAPLAN, *Dreams Are Letters from the Soul:*
*Discover the Connections Between Your Dreams and Your Spiritual Life*

Dreams which are not understood are like
letters which are not opened.
—*The Talmud*

The capacity to dream, the capacity to envision, and the capacity to imagine are all connected and directly allied to our capacity to develop spiritually. When we dream, visualize, and imagine, we see with an inner eye, and we have access to an inner knowing that has a direct conduit to collective consciousness.

Much of human interaction and endeavor depends upon the imagination and on our relationship with the forward-pulling motivation of the dream. To feel compassion for another means being able to imagine the nature of their suffering. To move in the direction of a happier and more harmonious way of living means being able to imagine what that life would be like in it. To know from a place of soul depth which way forward is right for us demands a combination of imagination and intuition (which is explored in the next lesson).

Many traditions foster the development of the imagination through prayer and ritual, as in Tibetan Tantric meditation, where the deity is visualized and merged with, or in Native American communing with animals and birds ("hearing" and "seeing" their messages). In contemporary spirituality, there is an emphasis on creative visualization as a

69

tool for shaping reality, and our ability to do this depends upon our ability to actively imagine.

In modern times, the fields of spirituality and psychology meet in the study and experience of dreaming. The numinous nature of dreams confounds logical analysis. Psychologists working with dreams cannot avoid encountering a mysterious level of experience in which the dream shows uncanny percipience and wisdom. Dreams often include archetypal symbols of which the dreamer may be unaware in normal waking life but that mysteriously match the dream content with the dreamer's reality.

Spiritual practitioners gain depth of perception, objectivity, and analytical skill by working with dream content psychologically. Becoming acquainted with your dream life and consciously developing your imagination is a central element in developing an independent spiritual practice. Your dreams reflect your psychological state and are a form of spiritual guidance. Both your dreams and your waking imagination are tools to help you navigate life with holistic skill. They allow you to listen to both your conscious and unconscious intelligence, and to perceive events from non-ordinary levels of awareness.

## THE HISTORY OF DREAMS AND
## DREAM INTERPRETATION

Throughout much of human history, people have considered dreams to have spiritual significance. Dreams have been thought of as messages from the other world—from God, from spirit guides, or from ancestors. Dreams have been a foundation of culture for many societies—a fundamental source of information that sometimes assumed a primary role in collective decision making. For the ancients, dreams were the vehicle through which the gods spoke to humans to predict the future or give commands.

The first recorded dream interpretation occurs in the epic Sumerian poem *Gilgamesh*, which tells the life story of the legendary king whose dreams were seen as prophecy and used to determine action.

The role of dreams in giving survival information is most famously seen through the Biblical dreams of Joseph. In addition, Solomon, Jacob, and Nebuchadnezzar were all visited in their dreams by God or by prophets who helped guide their decisions. The Talmud, written between AD 200 and 500, includes more than two hundred references to dreams. The Ancient Egyptians, Greeks, and Chinese all practiced dream incubation (the encouragement of powerful dreaming) through special rites, such as fasting, prayer, and sleeping in dream temples.

These beliefs are still found in nonindustrial cultures. For example, the Turkana of Kenya believe that it is through dreams that God speaks most clearly to humans, and it is through dreams that they get crucial information about rainfall.

In shamanic traditions such as those of the Native Americans and the Celts, the dream realm is another version of reality. Dreams come from the other world, which is just as real as the waking world. Dreams connect the worlds—the physical and spiritual realms—and pull dreamers into the spirit world, crossing the boundaries of time and space that inhibit our knowing.

While societies have differed in their beliefs and emphasis on dreams, the oldest and most pervasive cross-cultural belief is that dreams come true and should be heeded as a form of prophecy.

Somewhere between the ancient world and the Middle Ages, opinions about dreams began to diversify. Aristotle (fourth century BC) may have been the first to say that dreams were not a form of divination and were not particularly useful. He thought they were simply produced by the body as a byproduct of physiological processes during sleep, and by the imagination as an attempt to process the day's experiences. However, many centuries later, the medieval physician Galen (considered the father of modern medicine) used dreams in his practice and found them to be an important source of healing information.

In the nineteenth century several authors were inspired by dreams. Robert Louis Stevenson dreamed the whole story of *Dr. Jekyll and Mr. Hyde.* Upon waking, he told the dream to his wife, who encouraged him to write it down. With some initial reluctance, he did so, completing the story in a creative frenzy in less than a day. Samuel Taylor Coleridge was inspired to write *Kubla Khan* from a dream (although it was admittedly opium influenced). In general, though, dreams were considered a romantic notion, and most scientists thought they were not worth studying or paying any attention to.

Our collective relationship with dreams went through several phases during the twentieth century. The first modern person to understand their relevance was Sigmund Freud, who called dreams "the royal road to the unconscious." Freud considered that dreams needed to be interpreted for their coded messages about suppressed psychological material, and that the unconscious created the dream image to fool the conscious mind into letting the information through.

Jung disagreed with this approach, instead seeing the dream image as the language of the unconscious. He considered that the dream was wise and that its images were exactly what the unconscious wanted to show. In his memoir *Memories, Dreams, Reflections,* Jung wrote about the development of his work after he parted ways with Freud:

> *I avoided all theoretical points of view and simply helped the patients to understand the dream images by themselves, without application of rules and theories. Soon I realized that it was right to take the dreams in this way as the basis of interpretation, for that is how dreams are intended. They are the facts from which we must proceed?*

He also wrote, "To me dreams are a part of nature, which harbors no intention to deceive but expresses something as best it can."[3]

Jung was the first person to identify the collective unconscious—the home of the archetypes. In his view, the unconscious of each individual

---

2. C. G. Jung, *Memories, Dreams, Reflections* (London: Random House, 1974), 194.
3. Ibid., 185.

is connected by a kind of psychic umbilical cord to the unconscious of the collective, which is in turn created by all our unconscious minds. The collective unconscious operates in a language of archetypes—mental images and imaginary beings that help us understand our life processes. These images, often appearing as symbols, can be seen in art, Tarot cards, mythology, and fairy tales. Today the archetypes show up as characters and plot lines in movies and on television, and in the celebrities we collectively focus on, projecting elements of our own shadow.

Held within the part of the psyche Jung termed "the shadow" are both positive and negative qualities that we don't consciously identify with but that are part of the wholeness of human experience. We try to live safely yet we are fascinated by the extremes of rage, beauty, passion, foolishness, and power writ large in the tabloid version of celebrity lives. Success—in the arts, sports, business, or society—compels our gaze because it evokes our own inner dream of fully expressing life through the fragile, ephemeral, effortful vehicle of the human body and psyche. The human story is vast and multidimensional, but at the same time it is limited, private, and intimate, and at essence centers on one thing: love. We know we will die, yet to function we have an ego that cannot genuinely conceive of no longer existing. The archetypes exist to help us process and cope with these wildly fluctuating and eternally confounding complexities of existence.

Examples of archetypes are:

1. Personifications such as the mother, the child, the magician, the king, the wise old man, the hero, the seer, and the goddess.
2. Symbols from the natural world such as the star, the sun, the river, the mountain, the desert, the tree, and the forest.
3. Figurative symbols such as the cross, the spiral, the swastika, and the circle.
4. Experiences like birth, death, failure, ecstasy, competition, and falling in love.

Jung thought that the ultimate goal of a human life was to individuate. Broadly put, this means becoming yourself, free of the inhibiting effects of psychological complexes derived from conditioning and prior experiences. When individuation occurs, one becomes able to live one's life fully, free from fears and anxieties, and petty mental obstructions.

Jung's idea of individuation has many parallels with the Eastern idea of enlightenment. Jung believed that if you learned how to understand your own dreams—a process usually needing the help of a skilled guide such as a psychotherapist, at least at the beginning—you would naturally individuate, meaning that you would come to know yourself clearly and be able to live fully in your own authentic way.

Beginning in the 1920s, Frederick (Fritz) Perls and his wife, Laura, developed Gestalt therapy. In this method, they developed a new way of working with dreams in which the dreamer enacted all the parts of the dream. Fritz Perls believed that the dream was a representation of the current or general state of the dreamer, and that by inhabiting all the roles in the dream, the dreamer would reintegrate his or her projections or split off parts of the self. In this way, the dreamer would come to understand the dream as a summary of his or her state, and achieve psychological wholeness and personal understanding.

At the scientific level, dreaming gained more credence when researchers discovered rapid eye movement (REM) in 1953. For the first time, the physiological level of dreaming was understood. Later research in sleep deprivation showed that subjects suffered more fatigue and loss of well-being when deprived of REM-level sleep, so it was proven that dreams happen and that they are important to health.

Further developments of dream studies occurred in various post-Jungian schools, including archetypal psychology (working with the mythic level of the dream), transpersonal psychology (the spiritual and mystical dimension of the dream), and process-oriented psychology (the dream body and the shamanic aspect of dreaming). There is considerable crossover within these disciplines, and most well-trained psychotherapists today are versed in several dream work techniques.

## DREAMS AND SPIRITUAL PRACTICE

You can see from this history why I've included a lesson on dreams in this book, and why I consider that paying attention to your dreams is a fundamental aspect of independent spiritual practice.

I love dreams. I find the dream realm fascinating. After thirty years of watching my own dreams and twenty years of studying other people's dreams, I still can't define what the dream world is and where dreams come from. I have heard so many extraordinary dreams and stories about the relevance and perspicacity of these dreams that I now think the dream realm utterly defies definition. The collective imagination of the life force as expressed through dreams is so gorgeous and complex that describing it with the limitations of spoken language is impossible.

Dreams take us into both the mystery of our own soul consciousness and of the collective, and into the mystery of all human life. When we dream, when we talk about dreams, and especially when we try to understand dreams, we have to do so with a spirit of great humility and wonder; we are in a realm that operates on rules different from those of everyday life, a realm that is numinous, a realm that can give us experiences that we cannot fit into our usual, personal, egoistic version of reality.

To learn your own dream language, you really have to check your ego, preconceptions, wishes, and desires at the door, and it's not that easy to do. That's where a skilled therapist can help. I daresay that one can learn one's own dream language and get a lot from one's dreams without guidance, and there's a list of titles at the end of the book to help with this. For myself, sometime in my late twenties my dreams became so awesome and quite shocking in their power that I had to get myself into therapy to try to understand them.

Not everyone is what one could call a big dreamer. If you are, then you owe it to yourself to explore this gift. Even if you're not someone who dreams a lot, you will still have some significant dreams in your lifetime. Paying attention to the dream realm creates more dreaming. As you develop a closer relationship with the unconscious, you will find you have a better memory of your dreaming. In time, many interesting dream experiences will occur that can greatly enrich your waking life.

Most of us suppress our dreaming unless encouraged, especially when young, because dreams can be scary to the immature ego and because mainstream culture does not integrate dreaming at a conscious level. So when you start to pay attention to your dreams, you may have a backlog of information from the unconscious to process. Once the unconscious has brought itself up to date, the extent of your dreaming will usually calm down. At certain times in the moon's cycle and at certain times in life, one may not dream very much at all. Dreaming gets very active when there is a change bubbling up either in your personal life or in the collective unconscious, or when you are processing a change that has already happened.

There are many levels of dreams. The following descriptions are types of dreams that I have experienced myself and that people I have worked with have experienced. There are several ways of talking about dream levels, and this is just a start for this lesson. A dream will often involve several levels, sometimes moving from one to the next within the same dream. Dreams often have three phases, within the same night or on separate nights, with each phase telling the same story in a different way, and with increasing complexity and depth.

The following levels of dreams fall into three loose categories: daily life dreams, psychological dreams, and transpersonal dreams.[4]

## DAILY LIFE DREAMS

1. **Processing Recent Events on the Personal Level**
   You have a really busy day, and that night you dream of a mishmash of events from the day. Even if it seems banal, some of the dream content may show you something you

---

4. My development of these dream categories was influenced by the pioneering work of two notable teachers on dreaming, Connie Kaplan and Arnold Mindell.

were unaware of while you were awake and in the thick of it all.

2.  **Processing Current/Future Events on the Personal Level**
    These dreams range from the classic anxiety dreams of being late for an exam or being naked in the street to minor prophetic dreams of the car breaking down or of you having a fight with someone.

## PSYCHOLOGICAL DREAMS

1.  **Dreams About Relationships**
    These dreams often include communication with people you know. You might dream you are on the phone with a friend or family member. These dreams are usually a hint that you need to communicate with that person or that there is something about the relationship that you are not acknowledging. Interestingly, dreams in which you fight with someone do not necessarily mean you have suppressed anger. Sometimes fighting in a dream is simply about needing to make a stronger contact with the person (and yes, sometimes it *is* about suppressed anger).

2.  **Sexual Dreams**
    A sexual dream doesn't necessarily mean you want to have sex with the person in the dream, and it often doesn't. (Everyone can heave a sigh of relief, as inappropriate sex dreams are one of the most common types of dreams that people have difficulty accepting.) What it might mean is that you want to be more intimate with that person, which could mean telling him or her something that's on your mind or listening more carefully to something he or she is trying to tell you. It might also mean that that person has a quality that you want to get closer to—one that you want to symbolically get into bed with and develop more within yourself. Women struggling with career

challenges often have sexual dreams involving successful men, and men needing more feeling in their lives will dream about having sex with emotional, sensitive women.

3. **Dreams About Parents**
Up until the age of about forty, dreams about parents are usually quite prevalent. After that stage, unless you still need to do a lot of work on your parental projections, they become more infrequent. But when a parent dies, there is usually another phase of integrating the relationship, and this will most likely mean having some parental dreams.

4. **Dreams About Children**
These dreams may be about your children, or they may be about creative projects or responsibilities you have.

5. **Dreams About Your Shadow**
Shadow dreams, which are often combined with relationship dreams, involve a quality that you are averse to in waking life. These are the kind of dreams that you wake up and immediately try to forget, and yet they are the ones you really should write down. There will often be a repetitive figure who appears in your dreams and represents your shadow. A hysterical woman, a violent man, or a fat person is quite commonly found in this type of dream.

6. **Healing Dreams**
These dreams offer you information about what you need to do to balance yourself. They can be psychological or physical in their emphasis. They range from eating something in a dream and exercising in particular ways to recommendations for particular states of mind or actions. Paying attention to these dreams and following their guidance can significantly improve your health, both physically and emotionally.

## TRANSPERSONAL DREAMS

1. **Teaching Dreams**

   This category of dreams includes dreams about spiritual teachers, numinous places, and ecstatic experiences. If you are lucky enough to have these dreams, you'll know that they rarely need any interpretation.

2. **Prophetic Dreams**

   These dreams are for yourself and for the collective. They can be difficult to judge because you are dreaming into the future, which is not yet completely written. There are tendencies and streams of probability you can tap into, but the details can still change. And this becomes even more complex with the collective dream, which is not the same as the collective future. What one can say with these dreams is that you are dreaming about your hopes and fears or the collective's hopes and fears. It's more likely that a prophetic dream is genuinely prophetic when you dream about people you don't know well and you have no stake in their future. But some people have the gift of sight, and this will show through their dreams even when they involve a highly subjective territory, such as their own lives or those of people close to them.

3. **Soul-connection Dreams**

   These dreams can be some of the most awesome ones, but it can be difficult to return to your everyday life after having them. In these dreams, you fully connect with your soul essence and with your soul family, and experience a completeness of unity with other beings, animals, or places that you may rarely get to live out in waking life. There can be a tendency, especially when you first have such dreams, to try to replicate them once you wake up. You have to watch very carefully to see if replication is possible. If it is not, take a deep breath, recognize the gift you have been given in the dream, and let go of trying to manipulate reality to get the dream in waking life. This is where being able to manage your desire mechanism is an important piece of dream work. Not all dreams are meant to be acted upon. Many are simply experiences in and of themselves and are part of the wholeness of your psychic life.

## IMPORTANT THINGS TO KNOW ABOUT DREAMS

Your dreams are your friends, but they may not tell you the truth in the way that you understand it with your waking mind.

If a dream tells you to do something, sit with it for a while before making any kind of decision. Marie-Louise von Franz, a famous Jungian analyst, said that you should not follow the unconscious if it recommends action that is too expensive or dangerous. This is a good rule of thumb, but I would also add that life is a blend of waking perception and intuition/dream perception, and that it is often unwise to overrule a strong waking perception with a dream perception, however intoxicating and exciting the dream idea seems to be. If you can follow the dream symbolically rather than literally, then try that first.

Dreams are pretty much always more dramatic than everyday life. They tell their stories in loud, mythic language that we have to learn to decode.

## LUCID DREAMS

Lucid dreaming occurs when you know you are dreaming while you are still dreaming. Lucid dreaming was first termed such in 1913, and since the 1960s (the era of LSD, Carlos Castaneda, etc.) has attracted a lot of interest. This phenomenon has been observed for a long time, and even Aristotle made reference to it.

There are various techniques to encourage dreaming with lucidity, based on the idea that you can shape reality by conscious dreaming

and therefore make positive, willed changes in your life. I have mis-
givings about this approach, and I recommend you follow your own
natural path rather than trying to make lucid dreaming happen.

Most dreamers experience lucidity at some point, and it naturally
evolves as a skill if you pay attention to your dreaming process and
your personal development. You can still apply active awareness by
working on your dreams alone and/or with a therapist, but I think
that attempts to provoke lucidity with the technical, impatient, and
ambitious part of the mind are about as useful as similar attempts to
provoke spiritual enlightenment.

A common way that the dreaming process teaches you about
lucidity is the light-switch dream, in which you are wandering around
your house and try to turn on a light. You find that you can't press the
switch, and you panic and think that you will be stuck in the dark.
What is actually happening is that you are out of your physical body
and wandering around your house in your dreaming body. Eventu-
ally, instead of panicking, you say to yourself, "Oh, if I can't turn the
light on, I must not be in my physical body, so that means I must be
dreaming!" At that point, all kinds of interesting things start to happen in your dreams.

One of the main benefits of lucidity is the development in awareness that comes with it. This new awareness makes one more able to
tolerate and be alert in altered states of consciousness, which prepares
us for different states of being, such as those we experience when giving birth or dying.

⌒⌒⌒

## WHAT TO DO THIS MONTH

This month, pay special attention to your dreams. Write them
down every morning, and try to find a half hour to sit and let
them sink in. Think about what the dream realm is telling you.
With a soft, relaxed, trusting mind, ask yourself if the dream
is giving you information that will help you steer your course

through life with greater accuracy. Notice if any themes repeat regularly. Notice if you get dreams in threes or if there are three phases within the same dream, which quite often happens.

If you have a particular dilemma in your life at the moment, you can work with your dreams to resolve it and to know what steps to take. Just before you go to sleep, ask the dream realm for help. Do this every night for at least three nights. At the end of the time period you choose, look at all the dreams you have had during that period. Look for recurring themes and images. Look for overall tone. Look for how the conflict/difficulty is being expressed in the dreams and for the seeds of its resolution as shown in the dreams. If you still don't understand a dream, don't worry. Just keep paying attention and keep writing down the dreams. Over time, the dreams will usually become more and more transparent, and make their message clear.

# Lesson 7

# DIVINATION AND
# DEVELOPING THE INTUITION

● ◐ ◑ ○ ◐ ◐ ●

Know Thyself

—SIGN OVER THE GATEWAY INTO THE TEMPLE OF APOLLO
AT DELPHI, HOME OF THE ORACLE OF DELPHI

I n ancient times, when many of the words we use today were formed, the art of seeing into the future was seen as related to godliness and the realm of Spirit. The root of the word *divination* comes from the Latin word for a god, *divus*, which is related to *deus*, also meaning a god.

According to the *Collins English Dictionary*, divination is "the art, practice, or gift of discerning or discovering future events or unknown things." The word *divine* has several uses: it is a noun equivalent to the word *god*, an adjective meaning godlike, and a verb meaning to discern a future or hidden reality. It is also used colloquially to mean "excellent; delightful."

In the more secular times of the modern era, and aided by religions that have often wanted to own divine power, divination has been seen as a rather low-level activity, practiced by charlatans and misguided women trying to make a living by reading tea leaves. It's true that there is still a great deal of charlatanry in the realm of divination and that it is tricky territory. But it is nonetheless valuable and a valid part of the development of an independent spiritual practice. Divination techniques feature in wisdom traditions cross-culturally. It's not that doing it is wrong or a bad idea; it's the way you do it that counts.

## REASONS FOR STUDYING DIVINATION METHODS

1. Divination is a gift from the divine realm, from the spark of creation, the Source of all. It is part of our human birthright, one of the natural talents we have as human beings. It can help us live our lives with greater skill and awareness.
2. The lives of spiritual adepts show us that when you develop spiritually—when you meditate and/or pray and develop better self-knowledge—you naturally begin to develop the ability to read reality more accurately and to see into the future. We might as well help this process along by studying the matter consciously.

## DIVINATION AND SPIRITUAL PRACTICE

The ability to divine and the practice of divination have historically been seen as attributes of particularly spiritual people, and also as attributes that naturally develop in those who work to become closer to the divine through prayer or meditation. Stories abound of Tibetan masters and Hindu sages who can tell the future with uncanny accuracy. There are many tales in the Bible of soothsaying by holy men who were known as prophets (one who can see into the future and prophesy). Soothsaying means both wisdom (speaking sooth—i.e., truth) and telling the future.

If you pay very close attention to what is happening in the moment, you can gather a lot of information about what will happen in the future. A clear mind, a meditator's mind, is open to all possibilities and therefore can tap into the future without being clouded by fear or desire.

Since time immemorial, human beings have used divination to access deeper wisdom, get in touch with something closer to objective truth than our purely personal viewpoint, and tune in to the realm of information that is independent of time and place. Divination tools such as astrology, the Tarot, and the I Ching allow us a glimpse into a deeper layer of current reality; they give us a sense of future possibilities. But we have to be able to use these tools wisely—with patience and clarity—otherwise they simply serve to further confuse an already confused mind.

There are several elements involved in the wise use of divination tools (which, of course, include dreams, the subject of the last lesson). These elements are clarity of mind, emotional mastery, and activation of the imagination. I'll discuss these in more detail one by one.

## CLARITY OF MIND

A clear mind is not trapped in habitual thinking and limited by the expectation that everything will continue as it is now. Life is always in a state of change and flux, and a free and clear mind is able to surf the waves of this change with grace. It is not attached to maintaining a status quo that is actually not maintainable, but gives an illusory sense of security we often tenaciously cling to. It is this clinging that obstructs clear vision.

Meditation techniques allow you to enter the intuitive level of consciousness and to release your highly conditioned, subjective view of reality. When the mind is uncluttered by mundane thoughts and concerns, and is no longer dominated by lingering, unprocessed emotion, there is an experience of emptiness that is sometimes felt as a spaciousness and sometimes as a sense of mental relaxation.

If you can sit with this emptiness—this spacious clarity—clear thoughts can flow into your awareness. These thoughts will give you information about the present and the future. When you practice meditation on a regular basis, this spacious clarity becomes increasingly accessible to you in daily life, so you naturally become more intuitive.

When you use divination tools with this spacious clarity, you can interpret the information you receive with much more effectiveness, because you can see clearly what the cards, omens, or stars are trying to tell you.

## EMOTIONAL MASTERY

Emotional mastery means being able to describe to yourself what you are feeling, to respect the emotion and listen to what it has to tell you, and to give it some form of expression, which will then naturally release it. Much of the time, a healthy person does this instinctively, but we all have emotions we are comfortable or uncomfortable with, depending on our cultural and familial conditioning. Learning emotional literacy—how to understand and name our own emotional landscape—is part and parcel of psychological development and maturity.

Consistently working with the emotions in waking life and in dreams can help you develop emotional mastery. When you are the master of your emotions, your intuition can really develop. Being intuitive means seeing what is really there to be seen and not necessarily what you want to see. When you learn how to look beyond the tunnel vision of your fears and desires, a larger and more accurate picture becomes available.

We often overvalue hope and confuse it with positive thinking. Hope is a useful psychological strategy, but it is ultimately just as illusory as despair. Calm optimism is a better state of mind to cultivate and naturally arises as we develop emotional maturity.

## ACTIVATION OF THE IMAGINATION

There is a crucial connection between the development of the imagination and the development of accurate intuition. When you activate your powers of imagining—your inner eye—and when you learn how to relax your attachment to what you think you want, then you can begin to see clearly.

Imagination, creativity, dreaming, and intuition all feed each other and are related activities. Activating any one of these can, with the application of awareness, help activate the others.

## DIVINATION TODAY

Much of what passes for divination today preys upon the worries of people who are confused and destabilized by contemporary life. The millions who read their horoscopes on the internet and call psychics on the telephone are trying to handle their confusing lives while searching for the tools to do so. However, in many instances they become the victims of scams and misinformation. People are often desperate to hear what they want to hear and hungrier for reassurance than for the truth.

This rather pathetic trend is the surface manifestation of a phenomenon of deeper significance that may well represent a quantum shift in modern human consciousness: activation of the latent human talent for prevision and active visualization.

We know that the human brain has greater capacity than we generally use and that we are capable of developing stronger intuition. We have a pre-existing technology, handed down over generations, to help us. This ancient technology comes primarily in the form of divination tools and meditation techniques, and is part of a long-simmering cultural soup that now includes psychology, medical knowledge of brain physiology, and an increasingly creative society. This entirely new combination of knowledge, skill, and opportunity ushers in an era in which more and more people will develop reliable skills of precognition.

Such a shift in human consciousness may rival our descent from the trees or the invention of fire. As life becomes more demanding, we are learning to use both sides of the brain simultaneously. We have a new verb: to multitask. We had to invent that term because it's what we all do now, every day. Research shows that women are generally better at multitasking than men, and it's for that same reason—the ability to use various parts of the brain at once—that women have traditionally been considered more intuitive. But these days men, are learning how to multitask, and women are developing their abilities to focus and to process information systematically (abilities that used to be considered masculine). Across the genetic divide, the way we use our brains is changing.

On the popular level—where everything that is really grabbing human attention can always be seen—there are two major developments occurring simultaneously. Along with a veritable explosion of interest in divination, we are seeing a new activation of the human imagination, which is a precursor to the intuitive ability. (If you can't imagine, you can't see possible futures.)

Creativity has received a huge boost in recent years. Witness all the new creative writing courses and the new computer software that means anyone can make his or her own movie. It's easy to scoff and say, "Oh, but what amateurs get up to in their living rooms is no good," but that's not the point. The point is not whether we are all Steven Spielberg or William Shakespeare; the point is that whenever we create something that was not there before, we activate our imaginative capacity and enhance our brain function.

It is time to take the next step—to bring together these apparently separate social trends and to become more conscious about what we are doing. We have information from traditions all over the world, a collective storehouse of wisdom that has been created through the ages. We can now tap into this storehouse and access this sacred knowledge so that it can be used by all.

In times of great unpredictability, our intuition may be one of the best survival skills we have.

## METHODS OF DIVINATION

Given all of the above, you can see that as a part of developing your own spiritual practice and personal connection with the divine, and being all of the human being you can be, it is well worth developing a relationship with a method or methods of divination.

You probably already practice some form of divination. Most of us do, even if it is simply being aware of signs and omens. I'm going to describe different types of divination. If you are new to the practice of divination, choose the category that most appeals to you and go further into it on your own. If you are already experienced with some form of divination, this list may help you branch out into an area you haven't utilized before, or it may help you deepen your existing practice.

Methods of divination come in six main types.

## RANDOM METHODS

The most basic and original method of divination is that of randomly throwing objects such as stones or bones and divining the answer from the pattern in which they fall. The diviner harnesses apparent chaos to reflect a current reality and future potential.

This method includes a wide range of divination methods of varying levels of sophistication, including the analysis of tea leaves or coffee grounds, stones or runes, playing cards or the Tarot, and the I Ching.

The examination of tea leaves and coffee grounds is called *tasseomancy*. It is commonly practiced in Turkey and Egypt, and among the Romany gypsies of Europe.

Runes are stones with symbols on them. Their use developed from the ancient practice of throwing stones: the next step was to ascribe different characteristics to individual stones. These became the Runes. The Tarot can be seen as a further development of this principle but with pictures rather than simple symbols.

The I Ching is a sophisticated development of the ancient shamanic practice of throwing bones or stones, using yarrow sticks and later on, coins. The book of the I Ching integrates Chinese shamanic knowledge of the natural world with Confucian thought, describing the complex hierarchical and organized cosmology that was an integral part of the flowering of ancient Chinese civilization.

Making a curious marriage with sophisticated modern technology, these ancient divinatory methods continue to develop. The advent of computers gives us the potential for even more complex randomization processes. The internet abounds with an ever-increasing number of predictive websites based on random divination. There are also many computer programs available, such as the Oracle of Changes, a program that combines the I Ching with modern paintings designed to evoke the meaning of the hexagrams. Advances in physics have given a theoretical basis for understanding how random methods work, and the role that synchronicity and the nature of the observer (in this case, the diviner) have on outcomes.

## ASTROLOGICAL METHODS

Astrology is based on observable, repeatable information that has been gathered over many centuries. There are several techniques from different parts of the world, such as Western, Arabic, Chinese, Vedic (Indian), and Tibetan, that developed at various periods in history. Astrology ranges from the purely predictive and karmic (such as that contained in ancient, prewritten Indian horoscopes) to the more modern study of psychological astrology, in which astrology is seen as much as an inner phenomenon as an outer one: thus fated outcomes can be influenced by our personal inner work and our level of awareness.

The widespread popularity and growing acceptance of astrology has led to the inclusion of weekly or monthly horoscopes in newspapers and magazines that have an educated audience, such as the *Sunday Observer* in Britain, and *Vogue* and *Vanity Fair* in the United States. These columns are not simply for entertainment; they are written by serious astrologers who are acknowledged by their peers. Astrology has become big business, with some astrologers becoming wealthy from their books, computerized readings, and websites.

There are many excellent books and online classes available that can teach you how to interpret astrological information. In terms of finding an astrologer to consult with, the quality of astrological practice has improved considerably over the past few decades and there are now professional bodies, qualifications, and conferences. In general, it's a good idea to ask around for a recommendation. Remember that some of the most charismatic and well-known astrologers don't necessarily make the best counselors. It is becoming more and more acknowledged in the astrological community that training in counseling and therapy for astrologers is often essential for good, solid astrological practice. There are gifted individuals who can give a good reading without a therapeutic background, but there are also some astrologers who will just give you a laundry list of aspects and make grand pronouncements without being able to make the information useful within the context of your life.

## VISITING THE SEER

The seer is a human oracle: an individual who has the gift of sight. In the Western world, the most famous seer in history was the Oracle at Delphi in ancient Greece. This oracle existed as a source of guidance for hundreds of years.

The Delphic Oracle was an impersonal force that spoke through women who lived in a temple located at Delphi, northwest of Athens. The Oracle spoke truths that people did not always want to hear and had a large influence on ancient Greek life, as shown in literature and the arts. For example, in the great tragic play *Oedipus Rex* by Sophocles, a pronouncement from the Delphic Oracle underpins the entire drama.

Tibetan culture has a long tradition of oracles that is rooted in the pre-Buddhist shamanic religion of Bon. Still today the Dalai Lama seeks advice from the oracle, who is believed to inhabit the body of willing subjects on certain days of the year.

These days, seers are usually called psychics. In recent years the use of telephone psychics has become increasingly popular, but not without controversy and accusations of fakery and corruption. Psychics also work more openly now (for example, in New Age bookstores).

It is easy to be misled by psychics or seers who often speak with great authority. Remember that the information is always coming through the vessel of the speaker, which may or may not be truly clear. Readings can be distorted by the psychic's imagination, and by their own process and life experience. Sometimes their psychic abilities lead them to read the questioner's mind, and thus echo your own fantasy rather than offering a more objective kind of seeing.

Be particularly careful when working with this kind of divination. People who are drawn to be professional psychics are sometimes confused themselves and even psychologically disturbed. Some of them are genuine seers. Take time to get to know a psychic, and check out the depth and accuracy of their work before having a reading from them.

## DREAMS

As we know from the story of Joseph in the Bible, dreams have long been considered prophetic. Developments in psychology in the twentieth century increased both our collective knowledge of dreams and our interest in them. While there are still many who think that dreams are merely a chemical experience of the brain during sleep, the integration of the psychotherapeutic model into mainstream thought has given dreams more widespread credence than they have had since perhaps Biblical times. However, dream interpretation is not easy and requires dedication and skill. (See the in-depth discussion of dreaming in Lesson 6.)

## SIGNS AND OMENS

Signs and omens can be seen as a form of waking dreams using spontaneous synchronistic occurrences in the outer world as a form of divination. This divination operates on two levels:

- Being aware of the signs and omens that arise spontaneously as a mirror for your own reality.

- Deliberately asking the outer world to provide answers to queries. An example of this is the shamanic practice of asking a question and waiting to see what answer is brought by the natural world.

In the 1990s the best-selling book *The Celestine Prophecy* popularized the idea of signs and omens. Outside of indigenous cultures rooted in a shamanic worldview, this version of divination is still relatively rarely practiced. Often confused with primitive superstition, the idea of events presaging other events or offering commentary is usually ignored by mainstream Western thinking.

Here's an example of how one might use this awareness in everyday life: When I lived in Paris in 2002, I met a couple that had a dog, and they wanted to take me and my dog on a walk with theirs in the Bois de Boulogne. As we left my apartment building, a young boy fell off a wall, landing on his head. He screamed, blood flowing profusely, and his parents scooped him up, presumably to take him to the hospital. I noted that this had happened right at the onset of our expedition and wondered if it bode ill. Sure enough, another dog in the park attacked my golden retriever, and I had to intervene and get my dog away, with some difficulty. Then on the way home, we were nearly in a traffic accident.

Another time, driving from Los Angeles to Santa Cruz, a town I had never visited before, rainbows appeared in the sky throughout the four-hour car trip. There were so many of them that the continual display in the sky was awesome and even a little eerie. Almost one year later to the day, I moved to Santa Cruz, drawn there by a string of surprising opportunities that had unfolded over time and that I was open to, having noticed the rainbows.

Noticing these kinds of signs and omens involves using what has been called the second attention (second sight). This is the level of awareness that functions as a backdrop to the normal thoughts of "Where are my car keys?" "Must buy pasta for supper," "I'll call so-and-so tonight," and the like. Developing the second attention is a very worthwhile and fruitful pursuit. When we meet people who have good second attention, we feel it and may describe it as intelligence (but not in the sense of cleverness or knowing a lot about something), awareness, and being awake. People who don't have much access to their second attention seem asleep and often make for rather boring company. Lack of second attention can manifest as dullness or as tension. If you feel either of these in yourself, it is sometimes a sign that you are blocking your second attention, or that something is trying to make itself known and you are defending yourself against it.

## DIVINING TOOLS

The most commonly used divining tools are divining rods, which are used for finding underground water and lost items, and pendulums, which are used for making decisions and testing if something has a positive or negative influence. In each case, the diviner holds the tool in his or her hands and waits to see if it turns in a certain direction or makes some kind of movement. Knowing how to use these tools is a very valuable skill that is not difficult to learn. It appears that some people have this skill naturally, but I think that probably anyone can develop it. In my experience, divining tools are not accurate in terms of the mid- to long-term future, but they are very useful for the present moment and perhaps the very near future. They help us build the sensory intuitive function, where one feels in one's body whether or not something is a good idea, or whether a food or supplement is healthy for us. Our bodies are actually great big divination tools that give us clear information on what to eat, where to go, which direction to walk in, and whom to spend time with — if we learn to listen to the inner sense of well-being and to follow its instructions and recommendations.

## FATE AND PREDESTINATION

Is any event or meeting predetermined? I have experienced crucial meetings that appeared meant to be and that an awful lot of apparent coincidences had lined up to create. But I suspect that very little is certain. Many aspects of life appear to be up for change and adjustment, and if we are really paying attention, we can make those adjustments in a timely manner. Maybe the big things in life, the major experiences, are part of our karma and thus predestined in a sense, but the details seem to be largely up to us. It's here that divination can be very helpful, aiding us in making the best decisions we can make for ourselves, given our disposition and gifts. So if you get a "bad" reading, don't panic. It will always tell you how to avoid the worst and how to deal with a challenge to minimize it. And a difficult reading may operate as a warning that helps you change course in an important way.

## DEVELOPING DIVINATORY SKILL

● **If the Answer Isn't Clear**
Sometimes we aren't ready to know about something ahead of time, and sometimes we shouldn't know. If you don't get an answer to a question fairly easily, if the oracle gives you scrambled information, or if your mind comes up blank, stop asking. Come back later.

● **Have Fun with Divination**
Don't take divination lightly, but do have fun with it. The divine has a sense of humor for sure, and many divinatory techniques have a pleasingly childlike and humorous element to their usage and design. It's a fine line between play and creativity, and trivializing and not taking things seriously, but it's very possible to develop a lightness of touch with divinatory techniques. This means that you take them utterly seriously, but with a spirit of flexibility and confidence that allows your unconscious to really run with the images and information, and thus deepen your wisdom and awareness.

● **Don't Be Obsessive**
In times of difficulty, you may be tempted to overuse divination tools. If you find yourself becoming obsessive about using cards or pendulums, or visiting umpteen psychics, stop and give it a rest for a while. Wait until the previous consultation has lived itself out or circumstances have significantly altered before attempting to repeat any divination method.

In our rational culture, divination sometimes gets a bad rap. However, looking into the future is not just for the insecure or for people who want to control life. Divination is a time-honored way of navigating our way through life and being prepared for challenges before we are in the thick of them. It can help us make good decisions, and practicing divination in a disciplined and mindful way can help us develop our own intuition so that we are walking diving rods ourselves, able to sense future developments and make wise choices as a result.

In the final analysis, it is the awakened individual who has the strongest divinatory ability, from direct connection with the Source and an unobstructed relationship with inner wisdom, which is directly related to body sense. Astrology, cards, runes, and pendulums can help us in training our own perception, which is mediated through the physical body.

---

## WHAT TO DO THIS MONTH

This lesson has been an overview of divinatory techniques and our relationship with the intuitive function. For this month's homework, pick one method and practice it daily to get to know it better.

For example, if you want to understand more about astrology, get an ephemeris or astrological calendar and track where the planets are every day. If you know how to read your own chart, watch how it is affected by the current sky and see if you can detect any correlations with events, both inner and outer, in your own life.

If you feel drawn to the runes, the Tarot, or the I Ching, do a daily reading and read books about your chosen method.

If you have been enjoying working with your dreams and want to go further with this study, write down your dreams every morning and pay special attention to how they signal future events.

If you feel you would like to develop your powers as a seer, meditate daily and open up your mind. Ask questions about the near future and see if you get any information that later manifests.

If you want to develop more of the shamanic perspective, do a daily practice of going out into nature, asking a question, and seeing what happens to you immediately afterwards. Keep your second attention alert for information and hints from the other realms at all times.

Whichever divination technique you choose to work with this month, enjoy yourself, and make notes in your journal that you can refer back to later.

# Lesson 8

# SPIRITUAL PRACTICE AND THE NATURAL WORLD

● ◐ ◖ ○ ◯ ◗ ◑ ●

But ask now the beasts, and they shall teach thee;
and the fowls of the air, and they shall teach thee...
—JOB 12:7

One might say I had decided to marry the silence of the forest.
—THOMAS MERTON, *Day of a Stranger*

S pending time in nature is one of the most straightforward ways to find emotional balance and spiritual succor. When we spend time quietly in the natural world, we are able to enter the timeless and stable realm of wisdom that underlies our apparently ever-changing surface reality.

Of course, just being in nature isn't enough. Plenty of people live in the country but never really let themselves see and feel it, and many people visit sacred sites and natural wonders without allowing the essence of the place to permeate their being. You have to enter the natural world with patience, awareness, a soft mind, and a willingness to be taught and to be shown.

For the independent spiritual practitioner, nature is a primary resource. On a fundamental level, the body never lies, nor does the natural world. The ground beneath our feet and the sky above our heads offer us continual information, feedback, and inspiration. The creatures and plants that live on the earth are also sources of wisdom and support. The natural world, perhaps more clearly than any other influence, can reflect back to us our own inner truth and intuitive wisdom.

The life stories of independent spiritual practitioners are full of references to the healing and inspirational powers of the natural world. The Buddha came to enlightenment sitting under a Bodhi tree in a forest in northern India. He had encounters with wild animals that taught him deep truths about the nature of reality. Jesus spent forty days and forty nights in the desert to gain his realization of the spiritual truths of existence. The Catholic mystic Thomas Merton spent as much time as he could in his hermitage in the forest, a mile from the monastery he officially lived in. Tenzin Palmo spent twelve years living in a cave in the Himalayas so that her quest for wisdom would be unobstructed by the distractions of urban life.

In the Taoism of China and Korea, one of the most persistent and intact independent spiritual traditions, modern-day Taoists spend long periods, sometimes their whole adult lives, living as hermits in the mountains, communing with and learning from the natural world. And in tribes all around the world, the notion of a retreat or vision quest in the natural world is a crucial element in both adolescent initiation and in periodic spiritual renewal.

In the shamanic traditions found in many cultures, animals, birds, plants, trees, weather patterns, and the cycles of the sun, moon, and stars are the prime ingredients that weave the fate and the consciousness of human beings into the greater web of life. The natural world is seen in a literal sense as it is: as rocks, clouds, rushing water, birds, and beasts. All of this is also seen as the visible manifestation of the deity that governs existence. It is the vehicle through which the Great Spirit shows itself and communicates with human beings.

In the Native American and Celtic traditions, the role of the natural world as a spiritual force has been explored in great depth. The spiritual leaders of the Native American tradition have a sophisticated understanding of the symbolic meanings of animals and birds, and the energies of plants and trees. We inherit a parallel mapping of the symbolic reality of the natural world in the Druid/Celtic/pagan tradition of Northern Europe, as well as rituals to celebrate the notable moments of the seasonal year. The solstices, equinoxes, and cross-quarter days are the junctures that mark both community life and individual maturation.

We only have to look around us to see what happens to our collective spiritual health when we remove the natural world as an influence. Instead of paying homage to the world of nature, the industrialized world worships human-made objects. Instead of spending Sundays at church or in the country, modern people spend Sundays in front of the television or at the shopping mall. While the explosion of labor-saving devices has had many liberating repercussions (the lives of women in particular have been enormously freed up or can be, if the right choices are made), this has come at a huge price in terms of our collective well-being. We have growing epidemics of depression and obesity (both of which are often unconscious attempts to get closer to the ground) that clearly occur along with industrialization and increased luxury. Or to put it the other way, these diseases occur when we collectively turn our back on the natural world and the wisdom it reflects back to us, and when we ignore the natural rhythms of life.

## SPIRITUAL PRACTICE AND NATURE

To develop spiritually, and to grow in wisdom and maturity, the guidance and solace of the natural world is essential. The question is how to maximize one's contact with the natural world when leading the busy lives most of us lead today.

### DAILY PRACTICE

As complex electromagnetic and emotional beings, we need to experience grounding and communion with the natural world on a daily basis. Working out in a gym may help build your muscles, but walking through fields, amidst trees, or on a beach will give your physical body exercise and at the same time soothe your mental and emotional bodies.

Find the time to sit every day, even for a few minutes, and observe the natural world. Simply observe the clouds in the sky, the moon rising, the birds flying overhead, the berries growing on the bushes, or the new shoots of grass on the ground beneath your feet. If you live in a city, visit a park or garden. If this isn't possible, then take some time to really look at the sky. Rest your eyes on the nature that you have access to and simply *watch*.

Over time, you will be taught everything you need to know about the ways things really happen in life. You will learn about the value of timing, about how to move fast when the energy is with you, and about how to step back when it is time to mull over and to gestate. You will feel how nature is fundamentally happy, and how this happiness runs through everything at a cellular level as a constant undercurrent, and you will be able to tap into this at will, even when life is hard. You will feel the bubbly ecstasy of spring, the pushing of the sap upward in the tree and out to the new branches and leaves, the sheer joy of being a rabbit and bouncing through high grass in midsummer, and the freedom with which a hare bounds across fields stripped of corn in August. You will know how it feels to be a tree when she sheds all her leaves — how utterly liberated and free she feels. You will feel how deeply content nature is to fold back in on itself in winter and how peaceful the body of a dead bird is, lying in the snow.

There is no shortcut to this knowing, but daily experience of the natural world will take you there.

## RETREAT AND VISION QUEST

Occasional periods of deep and uninterrupted immersion in nature can catapult us forward in our understanding of our own lives, our life path, and the perennial, spiritual truths of life. One of the very best things we can do for ourselves is to go on a retreat or vision quest — to go into the wilderness far away from the noise and psychic clutter of our everyday lives. Ideally, take at least a week, but if this isn't possible, even twenty-four hours in the wilderness can be life-changing.

In Lesson 9, I go into the topic of retreat and vision quest in much greater detail, and give instructions for how to do a twelve-hour (dusk to dawn), a twenty-four-hour, and a three-day quest.

# THE NATURAL WORLD AND THE CYCLES OF LIFE

Spending time in the natural world offers us an initiation into the natural processes of life, and if we keep paying attention, it gives us a lifelong education that continually deepens. Birth, sexuality, death, gain, loss, and illness—all these life events become more understandable and more psychologically manageable when we have a strong relationship with nature. The mysterious gateways of existence don't lose their power to evoke awe, but they do become more familiar and less frightening.

Familiarity with the natural world helps us come to terms with death. If you truly observe a dead animal or bird with clarity and without sentimentality, you see peace and release. If you really pay attention as trees lose their leaves in autumn, you feel a kind of shimmering ecstasy, a liberation.

When we tune in to the cycle of the year and the cycles of life, we can cope with fluctuations of activity and energy in our own lives more readily; we become more patient and more skilled in our timing. This is an incredibly useful ability to develop, and it is often missed in today's world. Much of contemporary culture is infected with a commercial zeal that insists on growth and movement all the time. There are all kinds of life gurus, exercise and dietary experts, and New Age teachers who encourage people to push and to strive without ceasing. This doesn't work. For the most part, nature goes to sleep at night (and sometimes during the day), goes slowly when the day is at its hottest, and shuts down almost entirely in the coldest months. We are creatures of nature, and if we don't let ourselves take our own time, we get out of balance and stop living our own lives with truth and clarity.

Conversely, we can become stuck through laziness, inertia, and fear, and refuse to let the natural cycles of rebirth and renewal act in our lives. Being awake to the renewal part of the cycle means having the courage to change, to accept the onrush of new information and inspiration when it comes, and to notice the clues that the pattern of our life is ready to change. Nature can help us move forward fearlessly, both by mirroring for us how new life emerges and through direct help. Nature can give us courage, and it can also give us information about how and when to act.

## HOW NATURE SPEAKS TO US: ELEMENTALS

The prime, most fundamental beings and guardians of nature are the elementals. The elementals live in and around the primal sources of the natural world: air/wind, fire/lightning, water, and the earth itself. They used to be more visible to humans than they are today (as were all the nature spirits), and some of our knowledge of them comes down to us in myth and legend, and in ancient systems, such as the herbal tradition and the Tarot.

One way of understanding elementals is to say that they are a differentiated energy picture emitted by the primal source. They appear as entities that are sometimes human in characteristic and that represent the essence of the energy stream of the primal source they arise from. This energy stream has layers, or levels, of differentiation, and on the most differentiated level appears as the specific *deva*, or nature spirit, of an actual plant, body of water, or rock.

We can witness and communicate (to varying extents) with all levels of elementals, from the raw force of a volcano to the specific frequency, for example, of the pine tree deva. Fairies are a particular form of nature spirit that primarily dwell in and emanate from flowers, and flowering trees and bushes. All traditions have their stories about nature spirits; you can learn a great deal about a region by reading up on the legends about its elementals.

All the elementals are different, depending on their locale and type. They vary in size from very large to extremely small. Some of them like to communicate with human beings, particularly with people who are respectful and who are aware of them. Conversely, some prefer to communicate through grand action and rarely, if ever, offer a direct communication with an individual. The elementals like to be recognized, and legend and contemporary anecdote inform us that they can be extremely helpful to individuals who pay them respect and honor their existence.

Although they are relatively eternal and constant beings, the elementals do change somewhat over time, as do all entities. They used to be closer to human beings than they are now, or perhaps I should say that human beings used to be closer to them. Their relationship with human beings is less harmonious now than it was in the past. For example, the elementals understand the need for human beings to take metals from the earth (they are one of the earth's gifts, after all), but they experience some distress when this is thoughtlessly carried out.

The elementals can be worked with, however. If acknowledged, they will often make adjustments to suit human beings. This was well known to the ancients and is still understood by people who live close to the earth, and it is the understanding that lies behind many of the ceremonies, practiced by indigenous peoples, such as rain dances. Propitiating the elementals to ensure a good relationship with the natural world was also a fundamental aspect of early ritual and remains so in the practices of many indigenous peoples and others who live close to the earth.

## FIRE ELEMENTALS

The fire elementals are fierce and passionate. They make things happen on a big scale, often suddenly and with little warning. Some fire elementals live deep inside the earth's crust and emerge occasionally through volcanoes. Fire elementals can also be met in actual fires. Spending time with fires, including the ones you light in your own fireplace, can give you a greater understanding of the sexual and creative energies of the fire elementals.

## EARTH ELEMENTALS

Earth elementals live in caves, in mud and dirt, and in the strata of rock. The earth elementals are stable, steady, and abundant. They create wealth: jewels, gold, and all the precious metals. Communing with the earth elementals can teach you how to create abundance in your own life, and doing a ceremony to honor them when you move to a new home will help ensure sufficient abundance while you live there. Thanking the earth elementals for abundance that you have received is a good practice to develop, whether it's putting a check on your altar for a couple of days before depositing it into your bank account, or doing harvest festivals in the autumn.

## AIR ELEMENTALS

The elementals that live in the air can be wild and unpredictable. We experience them primarily through meteorological events such as winds and storms, but you can also feel them as a gentle breeze or sudden gust of warm air. This can happen when you are thinking about something particularly potent or something that you need to pay more attention to. The air elementals are very much related to the realm of thinking. They move things and processes along, and are good to connect with if you want to speed something up or send something from point A to point B. They are also good with relatively impersonal communications.

## WATER ELEMENTALS

The elementals that live in water are very playful and joyous. In many ways they are the easiest to connect with as they have the most feelings of all the elementals and are therefore closer in temperament to human beings. Those that live in streams and around waterfalls (a favorite place for water elementals, as the energy there is particularly fresh and vibrant) are more personal and friendlier than the ocean elementals. (Although having said that, there are a lot of elementals who like to live on the edge of the ocean, at the beach, and on the incoming waves, and these elementals are very happy to communicate with human beings.) If you are feeling depressed or emotionally confused, spending time at places where the water elementals congregate (waterfalls, the beach, or riverbanks) can do a great deal to lift your spirits and clarify your feelings.

The subject of the elementals is large and relatively unresearched and written about in present times. Ancient myths and legends abound with information about elementals and are often the best source for further reading. In modern times, the Findhorn Community in Scotland became famous as a place where communication with the devic realm resulted in enormous vegetables growing in sandy, relatively infertile soil. Books on Findhorn and those by the Findhorn founders offer some interesting material on working with the devas. Michaelle Small-Wright's work is also interesting reading.

I recommend spending time tuning in to the elementals and letting them tell you what they are about and how they will work with you. To start with, get a handle on the different energies of the elements by communing with the fire in your fireplace, the earth in your garden, the breeze on your face, and the water in a small stream.

## HOW NATURE SPEAKS TO US: TREES

Trees have always been revered. The Celtic tradition in particular has some wonderful lore on trees. Trees are a great gift. They give us oxygen, timber, food, and shelter, and beyond that, they have a special energy that can teach, protect, and guide us. If you take the time to tune in to trees, you will be amply rewarded.

One practice is to look for your medicine tree. Walk around your garden or neighborhood and see if there is tree you feel really attracted to. It may not be the biggest or most beautiful tree, but it will be a tree that draws you to it. Sit for a while under this tree. Lean against its trunk. Let the energy of the tree—the stable, rooted, earth-and-sky connected essence of treeness—enter your own energy field.

The deep stability of tree energy can help you in times of transition or emotional pain. After you have chosen your tree and spent some time with it, you can look up its symbolic meaning in the old traditions and see if you can understand why it was this tree, at this time, that drew you in.

Go back to the tree as often as you can. You can leave offerings of cornmeal or small crystals. If you menstruate, you can leave some of your blood at its base. Stand against the tree, and let the back and then the front of your body mould itself to the tree trunk. Creating a bond like this with a tree can be very rewarding and can give you an anchor as well as connect you to a very particular source of earth wisdom.

You may find that certain trees always attract you more than others. For example, people who tend to support and help others are often drawn to oak trees, which are symbolically the trees of wisdom, reliability, and steadfastness. Sitting under an oak tree can be very helpful when you are in a period when you need extra support. Redwoods are lofty, spiritual trees that shoot upward, live a very long time, and link earth and sky. Standing in a grove of redwoods is energetically like standing in a natural cathedral.

All trees are protective, offering a literal protection from the elements. Some are fruitful, offering food. Some are beautiful, offering visual joy and wonderful smells. To find out more about trees, read books on the Bach Flower Remedies, Celtic and Druid lore, and the Native American tradition.

## HOW NATURE SPEAKS TO US: ANIMALS AND BIRDS

There is so much to say about animals and the spiritual journey. Those of you who live with animals already know how much their presence adds to one's life and how much they can teach us. Traditionally, spiritual seekers, from wise hermits to witchy women, had animal familiars—animals or birds who lived with them and played important roles. Fairy tales abound with the archetype of the wise animal that influences the fate of humans.

Animals represent the instinctual realm and the wisdom we can access from the oldest part of the brain, which is closely allied to our intuition. When you live with animals you begin to realize how clever they are. Their survival instinct gives them an uncanny ability to observe their people very acutely and shape their behavior accordingly. But animal abilities are not simply about staying alive; the long-term development of their survival strategies has resulted in a wide array of sophisticated skills, and areas of profound knowledge and expertise.

Some animals, both domestic and wild, have very developed feeling abilities, form lifelong pair bonds, and become exceptionally good parents. Other animal skills include long-range perception, hunting, night vision, camouflage, fighting skills and self-defense, home building, healing, community creating, and symbiosis with other creatures. There are many more animal traits, and all of them are components that are relevant to the development of a well-rounded and spiritually mature human being.

In the Native American and Celtic traditions, animals and birds have been closely observed over millennia. Their attributes have been incorporated into systems of teaching about the world and about the spiritual journey the soul makes through life. The Native Americans, Celts, and those in other earth-based traditions understood that animals and birds influence us on both the physical and metaphysical levels. Thus an animal or bird in the physical world can give you information if you pay attention. (For example, if you ask a searching question about your life and at that moment a grasshopper lands on your desk, it might mean: don't be afraid to take a leap.) At the same time, there are animal and bird spirits on the nonphysical planes that can help us. These spirits are known as totem animals in the Native American tradition and as spirit familiars in the Celtic tradition.

You may have dreamed about your spirit familiars. Certain animals appear in our dreams, often in particularly numinous dreams. You may become the animal in the dream. This is usually because you are learning a skill that the animal has perfected. For example, sometimes people dream of being a bird and flying. This is usually because they are psychologically at a stage where they need to develop more of an overview of their situation.

At other times the animal may give you a direct teaching. For example, you might dream of a lioness when you need to be more dignified and self-willed, or of a bear when you need to defend your cubs, or be solitary and follow your own rhythm. Even more explicitly, the spirit familiar may give you a direct instruction. Once, a wolf appeared to me and told me to follow a relationship with a man whom I had mixed feelings about getting involved with. The relationship was not without complications, but being with him took me much further and deeper along my path, and I learned things from him that were rare gifts. (There are stages in spiritual development in which one's comfort is not the priority, nor whether your conventional side is satisfied. If you want to develop spiritually and be all that you can be, this will mean occasionally making choices that make life on the surface seem more difficult rather than easier, especially in the first half of life.)

I highly recommend the animal realm as a line of study and practice. Particularly at this point in our collective development, integration with the animal realm is very helpful in generating physical well-being and developing grounded intuition.

⸺ ∞∞ ⸺

## WHAT TO DO THIS MONTH

This month there are four exercises. This is not as much work as it sounds, as they dovetail into each other.

1.  Do the daily practice on page 101, being receptive to the sights and sounds of the natural world around you.
2.  Find your local medicine tree and get to know it.
3.  Tune in to the animal realm more deeply. If you have animals, spend some time simply being with them. See what they have to teach you. Open your heart to their wisdom. And at the same time, ask your dreams for information from the realm of spirit animals and birds. If you already have a sense of a totem animal or spirit familiar, spend

some time meditating on it or them. Activate the power of your imagination to deliver useful messages from your animal guides.

4. In preparation for next month's lesson on the vision quest, do a short shamanic walk. Go outside, and in a ten- to twenty-minute walk, see what nature shows you. With a soft and open mind, just see what grabs your attention and what unexpected things happen. Usually on a shamanic walk, one opens to everything, but for the purposes of this lesson, put a special focus on the natural world, and notice how you interact with and experience animals, birds, plants, and trees. Notice what happens with the elements, with the temperature, and with the breeze, and observe the relationship between your thoughts and the weather.

# Lesson 9

# SACRED TIME ALONE:
# VISION QUEST AND RETREAT

● ◑ ◐ ○ ○ ◑ ◐ ●

Nowhere can a man find a quieter or more untroubled retreat
than in his own soul.
—MARCUS AURELIUS, AD 121–180, ROMAN EMPEROR, AD 161–180

O ne of the hallmarks of the life stories of independent spiritual practitioners is time spent alone in retreat or on a vision quest. At some
point on the journey, you have to get deeply in touch with your inner
voice. Being alone, especially in nature and the silence of wide-open,
empty spaces, is one of the most potent and effective ways to do this.

A vision quest is a tremendously powerful method for unlocking
stuck places in the psyche and for accessing one's inner truth. It is
very likely that a vision quest or retreat will bring you realizations
about choices you have made in the past and about choices you
should make in the future. On a vision quest or retreat, a particular
mental clarity is available that the normal distractions of everyday life
tend to interfere with. You may access information about past lifetimes
and about your soul purpose in this lifetime.

Illness is a kind of spiritual retreat, and in taking one step back
from the world, a different kind of consciousness operates. For many
people, illness is their only experience of spiritual retreat in their
whole lifetime. While I don't want to judge the validity of illness as a
way of accessing different states of consciousness (sometimes it may

be the only way), there are benefits to consciously choosing to go on a retreat, particularly when you feel a lack of clarity or a need for a tough decision. If you don't consciously retreat, even if only for a day or a weekend, you may get sick instead, as a way of giving yourself the time and space to make the inner shift your soul requires.

It makes sense to allow the time for that process rather than have it happen through illness, because the bodymind is sick (literally) of waiting for us to figure out we need to take a time-out from regular life.

## THE RHYTHM OF RETREAT

No matter what style of vision quest or retreat you choose to do, there will be a fundamental rhythm to the experience, which we can divide into four stages.

1. **Adjustment**
   The first quarter of the time will be about getting used to the space and letting go of your normal state of consciousness. You can facilitate this process with prayer and meditation.

2. **Release**
   The second phase involves releasing the past. Old memories will come up, and there will often be a period of emotion, such as anger, sadness, and/or regret. When these feelings have been expressed, they are followed by a sense of release and acceptance.

   Then there will be an empty space where not much is happening—a liminal period right in the midst of the retreat in which you may feel hopeless, bored, tired, or simply open.

3. **Receiving**
   Next, there is a period of dreaming and inspiration about the future. During this time you will get information about what is important to you in life and the next steps you need to take.

4.  **Gratitude**

Following the third stage is usually a natural phase of feeling peaceful and grateful, and a sense of one's place in the larger scheme of things. Thoughts of love and generosity toward others arise, and at this point it is a good idea to note what you want to do to help and thank others, because sometimes we forget what we want to do when we get back into our usual, everyday lives.

● ◐ ○ ○ ◗ ◑ ●

Use your journal throughout the retreat. A lot will be coming up that you will want to remember when you make the shift in consciousness back into "normal" life.

Depending on your nature, you may struggle with the shifts within the retreats, and there may be particular stages you struggle with more than others. For example, someone who is used to being in control of their thoughts will find the first stage tough, whereas someone who has a more dreamy state of consciousness will find it easy but perhaps balk at the period of emotionality, be it sadness, rage, or another emotion, and find some resistance there.

Knowing the basic map of the psychic territory will help you avoid getting stuck at any of the interstices between phases or within a phase itself.

Sometimes you may find it difficult to move past a mental block while in a retreat, and this may arrest the natural cycle of the phases. If you realize you are blocked and your mind keeps going around in obsessive circles, try to relax and be patient. Self-kindness and self-acceptance will often allow the block to dissolve. If this doesn't work, you can make an agreement with yourself to leave an issue on hold and move on to something else.

If you come out of the vision quest or retreat feeling unfinished, you can work on the material later by working on your own, or with a therapist or spiritual counselor.

Sometimes in life we deal with very deep karmic and/or long-term incarnational processes that may take decades to fully unfold. Such processes will come and go in intensity, and the best guide to working with them is to follow the process itself. Know when to let go and get back into regular life; you can always come back to work on it later. You will not necessarily feel finished or complete when you come out of a retreat, but ideally you will feel you have done enough for now.

## STYLES OF RETREAT

There are many levels of retreat and vision quest, and the type that you find suits you best will vary depending on a combination of factors, including how much time you have available, where you live, and your current needs and reasons for the retreat. I'll start with the simplest kinds of retreat and work up.

### STAYING HOME ALONE AND TURNING OFF THE PHONE

This form of retreat is easy to organize if you live alone and in a place where you don't get many drop-in visitors. If you don't live alone, you can do it when your family or roommates are away. To not alarm your nearest and dearest, tell them ahead of time that you are going on a retreat for two, three, four, or however many days, that you wish to be left alone, and that they shouldn't worry if you don't answer the phone.

This retreat has the benefit of feeling very safe and cozy, which sometimes can allow us to open up to truths we otherwise might find threatening. We can deeply rest on this kind of retreat and allow our mental and physical batteries to recharge. It can be very healing for the nervous system when you stay in the safety of your own home, without distractions and in a consciously spiritual state of mind. Logistically this retreat is much easier to organize than going off into the wild, but it will not put you up against survival fears or existential fears in the same way being in the wild will do. Nor will it give you access to the deep wisdom of the natural world, but as an adjunct to those kinds of retreats, it is invaluable.

A home retreat can yield a great deal of wisdom, depending on how you use the time. You need to be disciplined and not turn on the television or computer, or use other distractions. You should have a clear program of meditation, diet, and exercise to structure your time so that you don't fall into the habitual behaviors that are bound to be triggered by being in your familiar space.

You could, for example, structure a retreat day like this: Get up; drink a glass of hot water; write down your dreams; meditate or do yoga or t'ai chi for an hour or so; eat a light breakfast; write in your journal; meditate again; go on short walk; eat a light lunch; rest; meditate; write in journal; take another short walk; eat a very light dinner; practice dream incubation and meditation before bed; and finally, go to sleep.

Allow yourself to have open, unstructured, dreamy time within the day. Use your journal to write down your thoughts and preoccupations. Notice who and what floats into your awareness. Notice what elements from your past rise up to be processed. Notice the territory your thoughts are lingering in and consciously follow them. At the same time, you can pay attention to the natural world by looking at the sky, watching your pets, or spending time in your garden, if you have one.

## VISION QUEST IN THE WILDERNESS

In the Native American tradition, the vision quest is a fundamental aspect of the spiritual journey through life. Undertaken first at adolescence, the vision quest is repeated whenever an individual feels the need for a deeper connection with the Great Spirit.

The vision quest at adolescence is an initiation into adulthood. It functions as a period of getting to know the newly forming adult self and listening for information about the future direction of the life path. It is also the moment when the child becomes an adult, taking full responsibility for himself or herself. Contemporary culture lacks conscious and spiritual initiation rituals, and as a result many of us stay emotionally and spiritually immature long into adulthood. We can make up for this by sending ourselves on initiation rituals as adults. The vision quest is a very effective way to do this.

Going on a vision quest makes you deal with and walk through your fears. Most of our fears—probably 99 percent of them—are entirely ungrounded. They arise out of the incompletely processed residue of past traumas, both in this lifetime and in past lifetimes, and are fed by our conditioning. At this point in human history, the culture of control through fear is particularly influential and widespread. Fear of terrorism, poverty, foods, illnesses, medical procedures, and extreme weather fill the newspapers and the television news. Fear sells, and we live in an almost entirely mercantile world. Every day, a new health fear is perpetrated in the guise of being information. Horror stories of dreadful (yet terribly rare) things happening to other people are the stock in trade of the nightly news programs and tabloid newspapers.

At some point you have to take responsibility for your own fear and your own vulnerability to being needlessly frightened. Nothing impedes spiritual, psychological, and creative progress like fear.

Most fear, boiled down, is fear of the unknown. When you go on a vision quest, you meet the unknown. There you will find some core lessons about the nature of reality and its relationship to your own state of mind.

Modern people tend to be uncomfortable in the world of nature. Accustomed to flush toilets and hot running water, to food and entertainment at the press of a button, we have grown flabby in the arts of survival. Spending even three days out in the wild by yourself will forever shift you out of these addictions and habits, and give you a sense of your own capability and strength. It will also put you in touch with your instincts—with the knowledge of survival and of living in the preindustrial world that is within all of us on a cellular level. It's very recent that human beings have been so separate from the natural world and from each other. Some of our problems with intimacy are also related to this fear of nature, this flimsiness in our relationship with the reality of life on Earth.

## DUSK-TO-DAWN VISION QUEST

If you have never done a retreat in nature before, the dusk-to-dawn retreat is a great beginning. It's also a good method if you don't have days to spend on a retreat but you really want to have a strong experience.

It's a good idea to do this, and all vision quests, with a friend reasonably close by, or, at the very least, to make sure someone knows where you have gone. On longer quests, you can arrange for someone to check on you every day, and bring you water or whatever you will need. If you feel confident about your survival abilities, then by all means be completely alone, but make sure someone knows where you are.

The first time I did a twelve-hour dusk-to-dawn retreat was with a group studying with Joan Halifax in Mexico. We were staying on the coast of the Yucatan, where there is a twenty-five-mile-long beach that stretches down into Belize. Our task was to walk all night on this beach, under a full moon. We were not to lie down, go to sleep, or speak to each other if we saw another participant.

Amazingly, I only saw a couple of people all night long. I had two moments of being frightened: once by a hallucination of a very large man who vanished when I stared at him and once by a pack of dogs. When I saw the dogs, I felt terrified, but I decided to imagine I was invisible. Oddly enough, the dogs immediately ran off the beach and disappeared, as if it were they who were invisible. I felt an enormous sense of accomplishment at having dealt with my fear imaginatively, and from then on the beach felt entirely safe to me.

It was very magical and mystical to walk slowly under the moon and along the broad beach, with the waves of the Caribbean crashing on the shore in a steady rhythm all night long. As the sky began to gradually lighten, I headed back up the beach to the meeting place. My mind was deeply relaxed and my steps felt effortless, even though I had been walking most of the night. Suddenly my perceptions fell out of their normal pattern and I "heard" the pulse of the earth, a steady slow beat of energy—the heartbeat of the planet. Hearing that changed me forever; it did away with a sense of disconnection from the ground beneath my feet that I hadn't even known I had.

At one point in the night, around 3 or 4 AM, I sat down for a while. I am pretty sure I fell asleep for a while, but that didn't matter. The rules are less important than the experience overall. One participant had to be rescued: he fell into a walking trance and never turned back, and someone had to drive almost to Belize to get him. They found him still walking purposefully south, oblivious of time or tiredness. This kind of thing is rare, but it can happen, which is one of the reasons why you have to tell someone where you are going.

I have also done several overnights in the forest, just with a sleeping bag and a bottle of water. This is relatively easy to do, especially when the weather is mild. Head into an area of wilderness and find a pleasant place, a spot that feels safe and secluded. Find a tree that looks protective and lean up against it. Make yourself comfortable for the night. Nap if you need to, but plan to stay awake as much as you can. If you like, you can take a journal to record your thoughts and any dreams you have. In the morning, offer your gratitude to the tree for protecting you, leave an offering of some cornmeal, and head back to your "normal" life, full of forest energy and tree wisdom.

The dusk-to-dawn vision quest will help you deal with any fear you have of the dark. Befriending the darkness is a huge step to take both psychologically and spiritually. Fear of death diminishes when we directly meet our fear of the dark and move through it. When we fear death less, we can live our lives more fully and be more of who we naturally are. When we grow comfortable with the darkness, our light can shine brighter during the day. And when you first experience the darkness as a warm blanket around you, you will feel a sense of relief deep inside your being. Relaxing into the dark and befriending the nighttime often brings wonderful breakthroughs.

## LONGER VISION QUESTS

For twenty-four-hour, forty-eight-hour, or longer vision quests, you need to be a bit more organized. Such vision quests are not everyone's cup of tea, so don't feel you have to do this to complete this course or to progress spiritually. You don't. It takes a lot of courage to do a vision quest or a retreat in the wilderness, especially on your own, and it is often best to do a vision quest with supervision or as part of a group anyway. But if you are reasonably comfortable in the wilderness, if you feel your survival skills are adequate to the task, and if you feel drawn to do this, here are some basic guidelines for doing a conscious and independent vision quest.

Make sure you have adequate shelter, clothing, and footwear if there is any chance that it will be wet or cold. It's generally a good idea to do a vision quest at a time of year when the weather will be mild so that dealing with the elements doesn't overshadow the quest. This is not about a grand survival adventure; it's much more about being able to tune in to your inner being in a peaceful and natural environment.

Traditionally one fasts throughout a vision quest, so you don't need to worry about bringing food unless you have a medical condition that precludes fasting (such as low blood sugar, diabetes, or a heart condition). I do not recommend fasting for more than three days, and it is imperative that you go into and come out of the fast correctly, eating lightly the day before and the day after the fast. When you break the fast, eat fruit and then gradually work up to food that is harder to digest. Do not eat dairy for one day or meat for two days after coming out of a fast. Also, if you have hiked a long way in to your vision quest spot, you will need to take some energy food with you, such as dried fruit, so that you can eat a little before hiking back out.

You need to have enough water on your retreat. If you are going on a quest for longer than twenty-four hours, unless you camp near a source of drinkable water, you will need to arrange for someone to

bring you water every day. You should make sure to have at least
eight pints of water a day for drinking and more if it is hot. In addition to your usual hydration needs, you will be detoxifying and will
require extra water to flush your system.

It goes without saying that it is only sensible to do a vision quest
with someone else reasonably nearby, and in an area that feels safe to
you. For example, don't do a vision quest where there are lots of
bears, especially when you are having your period. Having said that, I
do believe, and it has been my experience, that when one goes into the
wilderness with a clear and spiritual intention, the natural world is
very supportive and respectful. But you still need to keep your wits
about you. Perhaps one of the craziest things I have done in this kind
of situation was walk barefoot in a snake-infested jungle, but I had
been doing weeks of shamanic ceremony and fasting, and was in a
strongly altered state of consciousness in which I could feel the snakes
and had psychically befriended them. On the other hand, maybe I
was just very lucky!

As you probably know, the vast majority of wild creatures would
much rather stay out of your way, and as long as you don't provoke
them with stupid behavior, they will not do you any harm. In some
ways it is better to go to wilderness areas where there are no parks, as
the wildlife will be more afraid of you and won't associate you with a
possible food source. The fact that you will have no food with you is
also an advantage.

Areas that are especially good for a vision quest are places that
have been considered sacred by indigenous peoples. Deserts, mountains, forests, and some sacred sites are all places where you will find
the quiet and the wildness that give opportunities for spiritual breakthrough. Caves offer good shelter, as long as you know how to check
if it's the lair of some other creature! You can, of course, take a tent
with you, although I recommend sleeping under the stars if you can.

When you get to your chosen spot, look for eight large stones.
Lay them around you in a circle, one for each cardinal direction and
one in between each direction. This ring of stones is your protection

and marks your sacred space. You will sit within it for the bulk of your retreat.

Smudge yourself and the circle with sage and offer up a prayer, setting your intention for the retreat—for your calm, safety, and enlightenment—and saying you will do no harm to your surroundings or to the creatures who make their home there.

Then sit in your circle and pray, meditate, write in your journal, and watch for signs from the natural world. To do this, imagine you are living in a dream. Relax your normal thinking, analyzing mind. Soften your awareness and see everything that happens to you as part of an interlacing web—a constantly dancing pattern of reality. The ladybug landing on your finger, the hawk flying overhead from east to west, the moment when you are suddenly drawn to look up into the sky and see a cloud in the exact shape of a rabbit—all of this is symbolic and brings information; don't try to think or stress about what it all means. Feel the pattern. Notice what happens. Through your intuition you will come to know what you are being shown. Write down what happens as a way of anchoring your experience, just as you would write down a dream.

This is a very basic guide to a vision quest. I recommend you read further on the subject and talk to people who have done vision quests themselves.

## RETREAT AT A SPIRITUAL CENTER

Many spiritual centers, monasteries, and convents offer the opportunity to go on a retreat there, with your own quiet room, spending a weekend or longer within the simple lifestyle of the community. Some of these spiritual communities also live much of the time in silence. This can be an excellent way to have a retreat that is less physically demanding than a vision quest, but will nonetheless give you a time of spiritual rest and rejuvenation. The advantage of these situations is that you are also drawing on the collective, meditative atmosphere of a place where the practices of prayer and contemplation are embedded in the walls and in the daily life of the inhabitants. There may also be services and gatherings that will enhance your retreat, as well as the chance to discuss spiritual matters with the residents.

## A LIFESTYLE OF PERIODIC RETREAT

For the independent spiritual practitioner, retreat is a practice that is usually repeated periodically, when the need or desire arises. For some people it becomes a way of life, but this is not everyone's path. I find it valuable to take the time for short retreats several times a year, either coinciding with the new moon or with one of the ancient holy days, and taking two days out of "normal" life. Every few years, I find the time to go on a longer retreat.

The need for retreat varies at different times in our lives. Adolescence and menopause/andropause are traditionally times when people take a break or go on a vision quest to process the shift and to gain information about the next phase in life. For menstruating women, the period offers a natural space for a short retreat every month. There are also other inner cycles that draw us into retreat mode.

Learning how to read yourself and follow the impulse to retreat when it arises can greatly enhance your relationship with your deeper self, improve your psychic and physical health, and help you make good long-term decisions.

Whatever style of retreat you choose, by the end of it you should feel psychically ironed, as though a crease in your being has been smoothed out. This sense of clarification, renewal, and smoothness will carry you into the next phase of your life.

## WHAT TO DO THIS MONTH

Take some time this month, even a half day, to consciously retreat from your normal life to pray, meditate, and rest. During your retreat, use your journal to record your experience, and at the end of the retreat, record how long you spent in retreat and what it felt like overall. Answer these questions for yourself:

 Has this retreat changed any of your perspectives about your life?

 Did you access an inner knowing?

 Are you going to make any changes in your life as a result of this retreat?

# Lesson 10

# GRATITUDE, WONDER, AND ACCEPTANCE

● ◖ ○ ○ ○ ◗ ●

True knowledge comes of three things: a tongue which repeats the
name of God, a heart which is grateful, a patient body.
—AFLAKI,[5] *The Whirling Ecstasy*

Gratitude, wonder, and acceptance are closely related states of
mind and being. They all arise out of a love for life and a sense
that there is a meaning and a mystery to our existence. They are all
strongest when we have powerful experiences that open the heart,
when we let go of trying to control, and when the ego and the personality are relatively quiet and the soul speaks loudest within us.
Together, they are key ingredients in an ongoing state of spiritual
maturity, which is paradoxically also a state of innocence and childlike joy. They are inspired by and, in turn, generate each other in a
circuit of feeling and experience. If you feel any one of them, the
others will naturally come along, too. So if you want to be more
accepting, start with saying thank you. If you want to find more gratitude in your heart, go somewhere that provokes a sense of wonder (the
ocean or a cathedral, for example). If you want to feel more wonder
at life, open your mind to accept what is right in front of you, and

---

5. Aflaki was a disciple of Rumi's grandson, and he wrote several texts on
Sufism between 1318 and 1335.

you will glimpse the awesome perfection of everything. And you will feel profoundly grateful.

## GRATITUDE

"Gratitude is the key to joy" is a Sufi saying. In the Christian tradition I was raised in, it was a traditional part of bedtime prayers to thank God for everything you had received that day and for anything in your life you felt moved to express thanks for. The expression of gratitude is a feature in all the world's religions. In the 1990s the idea of the Gratitude Journal—based on the work of Sarah Ban Breathnach—was popularized by Oprah Winfrey on her television show.

A core piece of human experience that had once been part of mainstream daily practice had been forgotten, and we needed to be reminded of it. I am grateful to Oprah and to Sarah for reminding us that gratitude is such a vital aspect of life that can be deeply healing and liberating.

Gratitude is tremendously important, both in one's relationship life and one's spiritual life. It's a big part of having a glass half full rather than half empty. If you don't focus on what you've received, you tend to focus on what you haven't received.

Gratitude seems simple, but for various reasons it is an area of life that people often find awkward. How many of us have not written a thank-you note when it was due? How many of us resisted writing thank-you letters for birthday presents when we were children? How many of us spend more time complaining than we do being grateful, even when we lead lives of extraordinary plenty on all levels?

There are several reasons for failing to fully recognize gifts and to express gratitude.

1.  **A Sense of Entitlement**
    "My grandmother *should* give me a present. It's her job. Hey, I didn't ask to be born. So why should I write a letter back to her?" Or "The sun rises *every* morning. It's just sappy to give

thanks for that." These attitudes are allied to feelings of superiority and inferiority. Similarly, it's not fair. "They have so
much that they *should* give me some. It's my right."

2.  **A Sense of Grievance or Having Been Wronged**
    "I'm always doing stuff for her. Finally she buys me a measly
    cup of coffee. Does she think I'm going to say thank you now,
    after all the trouble she's put me through?" Or "I've had a
    really hard time. It's about time God/fate/the universe gave me
    a break."

3.  **The Desire to Stay Separate**
    If you say thank you, you are admitting that you needed to be
    helped. That means you have needs and are not perfectly
    autonomous and independent.

4.  **A Sense of Obligation**
    If you say thank you, that means you acknowledge the gift,
    which means you might have to give something back.

Dependent people, especially women and children, tend to suffer
more from the first and second reasons, and men and independent
women tend to suffer from the third and fourth. But we probably
recognize all these thoughts as part and parcel of our response, on
occasion, to situations where gratitude is called for. This is fruitful
territory to work on psychologically. It is also fruitful territory to
work on spiritually. How often do we play these particular mental
trips in our relationship with the spiritual realm?

The best way to delve into this is to start saying thank you a lot,
whenever you get the faintest opportunity. See where and when
resistance arises. Is it easier for you to say thank you to a beautiful
tree for gracing your view than it is to say thank you (and really
mean it) to the annoying colleague who does you a favor for once? Is
it easier for you to say thank you to your best friend when she sends

you a birthday card than to your mother-in-law (who you feel always criticizes you) for the one time she says your hair looks nice? How does it feel to thank the infinite, the divine, for a blessing that occurs in your life? If you experience resistance to expressing gratitude, whether to an individual or to the ineffable, inquire within as to the source of this reluctance—to the belief or feeling that obstructs you being able to say thank you. Then see how it feels to move past that block, and let your heart open with thankfulness for all the blessings in your life.

There is another level of gratitude, beyond being grateful for the good things, where we find the wisdom and the openness of heart to be able to say thank you for unpleasant and difficult experiences. This is where you say thank you for an illness that was really painful but left you with some wisdom you couldn't have come by any other way at that stage in your development. Or you say thank you to the traffic cop who gave you a ticket because you know you needed reminding about paying attention to boundaries and timing.

At the next level, we practice gratitude by saying thank you for everything, trusting that what we receive is part of our life journey and therefore somehow perfect. You say thank you even when you don't know what good, if any, will come of a situation, because you know that somehow it is part of the whole story of your life. You know that life itself is a precious gift of such multidimensional glory that there are not words or even deeds to fully express your gratitude for the gift of it.

Taking a step further, looking at the really big picture, we are able to expand and say thank you for world events that are devastating but part of the evolution of the heart and soul of humanity. (Now, that's a stretch, right?) This is where you recognize that the dark and the painful are as important as the light and the easy, that they are all colors of life and part of the whole. At this point you come close to a full integration of your being.

There's just one more step: Turn that expanded consciousness back onto yourself and feel grateful for all the darkness within your own being; for the resistance, the petulance, and the smallness, and for the ugly, mean little thoughts and actions that litter your days. It is all part of the gift of your life. It's part of your soul journey this time around. It's amazing how turning to these parts of yourself and thanking them for being part of your journey to wholeness transforms them into positive, joyful energy and appreciation for yourself and for life. The experience of feeling grateful for all of yourself, including the shadow, for acknowledging all of it for being somehow part and parcel of everything, gives you compassion and an understanding of others, and it makes it impossible for you to feel superior. Only those who hide from their own inner frailty, weakness, and meanness can judge others harshly. And only when you love and accept what you perceive as your own failings can you fully love and accept others.

So you see, gratitude *is* the way to joy and to love. It is the path we walk along to an open heart that can hold the whole world.

Gratitude is also the key to abundance in the material realm as well as in the nonmaterial joys of living. That's why all cultures have made a point of celebrating harvest time. It's natural to say thank you when beneficence comes your way, even if it is simply an apple from a tree. Make sure to be thankful for the small things as well as the large. That way you keep your energy field open to the flow of energy moving in and out. Gratitude for everything you receive, no matter how hard you feel you have worked for it, helps you stay clear of the traps of superiority and entitlement, which are both endemic spiritual traps in this time of extreme materialism.

When you are grateful, your heart is open, and you can receive all the abundance of love and wealth your soul needs. When you are truly receptive, you are filled, and then you empty yourself, giving to others. You live in a constant stream of taking in and giving out. There's no clinging. This is the essence of the feminine principle of receptivity balanced with the feminine principle of nurturing.

If you can find yourself in such a place of trust that you experience gratitude for whatever life brings, without any expectations or demands, you will be truly, unboundedly happy. And you will no longer feel separate from your own self, from the divine, or from the other beings in your life.

All this is why gratitude practice is fundamental and can be so deeply transformative. Gratitude for all things is one of the paths out of the wheel of karma. Once you see everything as a gift to receive, you stand in the center of the circle, the hub of the wheel, no longer carried up and down by the never-ending cycle of fate.

## THE GRATITUDE WORKOUT

This exercise takes place over a period of a month, gradually building in intensity. It's a powerful yet gentle way to initiate yourself into a deeper understanding of the power of gratitude to change your life.

- For the first week, every morning or evening (whichever works best for you), take a few minutes to write down five things you are grateful for—no more.

- The second week, write down ten things a day.

- The third week, fifteen things a day.

- The fourth week, twenty.

- At the end of the month, read through your gratitude writings and see what you think. What kinds of things and what aspects of life did you find you concentrated on? Are there any glaring omissions? What changes did this exercise bring in your perceptions of your life? In the actual events of your life?

If you want to carry on the exercise after the month is up, do so without limits.

## WONDER

Wonder is a word that encompasses several aspects of the spiritually aware life. On the simplest level, wonder is when you see a brilliant pink and gold sunset illuminating the evening sky, and your jaw drops in awe at the sheer unparalleled beauty of the natural world. Wonder is when you hold a newborn baby in your arms and marvel at the sweet, warm smell of its head and the petal softness of its skin. Wonder is when you walk into a candlelit house and smell bread baking in the oven, see a fire in the grate, and a Christmas tree surrounded by piles of brightly wrapped gifts.

It is easy to feel wonder and delight in these circumstances. But if your eyes are opened and your awareness is switched on, you will constantly experience wonder. Life is a nonstop display of beauty, whether it occurs in the simplest elements of the natural world or the most consciously created forms of art and culture made by human beings.

Wonder is a quality of fresh and immediate thought, untrammeled by expectations and preconceptions; wonder is completely in the moment. It is pure, it is unmediated, and it is spontaneous. It is a feeling that can sweep all other thoughts out of the way, and it cleanses the mind.

This is why it is so refreshing to spend time in awesome environments, whether a beach at sunset or a cathedral. I've spoken about the natural world in previous lessons, but what of the human-made world? Temples, cathedrals, palaces, and art museums can all take us out of ourselves and into this state of wonder. That's really what tourists are doing: refreshing their minds by being filled with wonder at the beauty of sites and sights. It might look as if they are logging notches on the belt of Things One Must Do and See, but they are in fact retuning their brains and emptying themselves of the petty concerns of the everyday round.

Places of worship are designed to provoke wonder and a sense of awe. They are designed to make your jaw drop when you walk in and see the splendor of the craftsmanship and the vastness of the interior space. In so doing, they trip you out of the habitual mind and straight into a sense of the awesome and unfathomable depths of life, and of the spirit that infuses all living beings.

Beauty inspires wonder and thus a sense of worship—of bowing down before something ineffable and glorious. So when we enter a cathedral, especially the great European medieval cathedrals built when the art of provoking awe was at its height, we find ourselves spontaneously in a state of worship, recognition, and adoration.

Sometimes people feel uneasy around the idea of worship, as if they are giving over something to a deity. Perhaps this stems from having felt damaged and coerced by organized religion. But perhaps it is also the clinging of an immature ego to a narrow notion of self. Worship of something apparently outside the self is good for the ego in that it keeps it in its place. It engenders a natural sense of humility, and this humility can help us make better decisions.

When you feel wonder or awe, you connect with the thing you feel awe about, whether it's a person, a field full of sunflowers, or a cathedral. So the spontaneous feeling of deep appreciation is, at its most heightened level, a connection with the ineffable and with the mysterious perfection of reality. And just because one recognizes the glory of something other than oneself doesn't preclude acknowledging those same qualities within oneself; indeed, it may enhance such a recognition. That's how the sense of unity arises, or at least it's part of how it arises. Just as you experience a sense of unity when you love and adore another person, you draw closer to unity with the divine when you allow wonder and awe to take you into worship and adoration.

## ACCEPTANCE

When we feel grateful, when we are in touch with the wonders of life, we can accept our fate, our age, and our nature. We can accept who and what we love and who and what loves us.

We can accept our natural spirituality and stop trying to force ourselves onto paths that don't suit us. Then we have a clear sense of how our spiritual inclinations can most fruitfully develop.

By experiencing this generosity toward ourselves and the unique pattern of our lives, we can accept others for who they are. But acceptance does not mean passivity. It doesn't mean rolling over if someone is mean to you or to others. Acceptance means accepting your own reaction; that is as much a part of the moment as anything else. Your rage at injustice is part of the Tao. It is part of what wants to happen.

Take a second to check where that sense of injustice comes from. Is it something you really need to defend? If so, go for it, no holds barred. Stand up for yourself and defend the defenseless. But if it is simply your nose being out of joint because you're not getting your way all the time, then drop it. Life is too short. Choose your battles wisely.

Acceptance of the whole play of life—the struggles and challenges as well as the peaceful moments and loving connections—is a large part of developing a functional, useful wisdom. As life stretches us and pulls us out of our limitations and into a larger version of ourselves, we find ourselves broadening, deepening, and stretching. We find the depth to accept the things we don't like, even when they appear to hamper our progress.

With acceptance, we recognize and embrace the great life lesson that when the way forward is blocked, it is because we have not yet completed the current stage. When we are grateful and filled with wonder, we can accept the body. We find the patience to accept the limitations of growing older. We realize that as a well-lived-in body grows older, it softens and widens.

There is more space now.

---

## WHAT TO DO THIS MONTH

Gratitude, wonder, and acceptance form a kind of mantra for moments or periods of difficulty. Remind yourself of them on a daily basis. Do the gratitude exercise on page 132. Watch where and when you find your heart goes hard and resists feeling grateful, when you find it impossible to accept what is happening or how someone is, and when you feel cynical instead of wondrous and open. Watch those times, discover what the triggers are, and love yourself anyway.

# Lesson 11

# SPIRITUAL PRACTICE AND THE MATERIAL REALM

● ◗ ◖ ○ ◗ ◑ ●

Call the world if you please "the vale of soul-making."
— JOHN KEATS, LETTER TO GEORGE AND GEORGIANA KEATS, APRIL 21, 1819

Most excellent man, are you who are a citizen of Athens, the
greatest of cities and the most famous for wisdom and power,
not ashamed to care for the acquisition of wealth and for
reputation and honour, when you neither care nor take thought
for wisdom and truth and the perfection of your soul?
— SOCRATES, QUOTED IN PLATO'S *APOLOGY*

Keats's phrase "the vale of soul-making" does more for me to sum up the reality and the purpose of life than any other. This notion of the world as sacred training ground, as a garden for the soul, resonates with the core of our experience. And Socrates's comment to the wealthy Athenian on our responsibility not to be overly swayed by the seductions of the material realm and the urge for power is as apposite today as it was when he spoke it nearly 2,500 years ago.

Taking these two quotes as our starting point for investigating the relationship between soul and matter, we see the world as a place in which souls are made, and that our work is to strive for our souls' perfection. Yet paradoxically, this very vale of soul making threatens us with endless distractions from the job at hand. How often does the need to make a living appear to conflict with the soul's needs, and how can we reconcile the two apparently opposing urges of bodily comfort and soul making? As a writer and spiritual practitioner, this is a question I have often confronted in my adult life, and for whatever reason, I have always taken the side of my soul, sometimes to the detriment of my bank account and my apparent material security. Yet it has always been my belief that in the long run, this is the wiser course, because selling the soul can cause terrible damage not only to oneself but also to each person one loves, encounters, and influences. But one must eat, and it is often the case that the demands of the material realm push the dreamer and spiritual seeker into life lessons that are exactly what he or she needs.

Finding a balance is often difficult, and in this highly material age it is all too common for people to sacrifice big chunks of their soul's needs on the altar of material security. Many people seem to be only aware of their need for material security, and allow it to dominate their lives to the extent that their creativity, individuality, and integrity are stifled into a coma of dullness and predictability.

What does it mean to sell one's soul? Why on God's good earth should it be the case that seeking material wealth so often involves ethical and personal choices that threaten the journey of soul making, the task of perfecting the soul? Apart from the potential for learning and the discrimination that comes with this challenge, we have to take into account the seductions of the material realm. Perhaps the clearest description of this comes to us in the Buddhist concept of the attachment process of human beings, who, incarnating into matter from the realm of spirit, become intoxicated by the joys of the sensual life and lose their bearings in a continual orgy of sense fulfillment. What we have is not enough. There are always more clothes to buy, bigger houses to purchase, and more exotic holidays to take. Some of the unhappiest people I have known have been among the wealthiest. They are still hungry, still anxious, and still afraid.

## BETWEEN HEAVEN AND EARTH

Independent spiritual practice is all about the conscious development of the soul as the mediating entity between the world of Spirit and the world of matter. The soul is the essence that incarnates into a human body and enables the will of heaven to be made manifest on earth. The relationship between heaven and earth, between Spirit and matter, is processed and experienced through the journey of the soul through life. And inevitably there are ups and downs on this journey.

There are the moments or even lengthy periods of sublime union and concord, when soul work brings you lots of money, when your intuition leads you to a beautiful home, when a journey goes without a hitch. There are also times of discord, when you struggle over financial demands that threaten your soul's freedom, and appear to limit or disable the soul's remit to create and make manifest the dreaming process of both the individual soul and the collective Spirit.

Given the tenor of one's personal journey, we get varying doses of the sublime patches and the difficult challenges. Never make the error, though, of equating material success with spiritual development. To say it's not that simple is massively understating the case. The ability to tolerate and to stay happy and generous under difficult physical conditions is a better hallmark of a perfected soul than just about anything else.

If we understand the soul to be the mediating entity between the spiritual world and the material world, we can see that the soul can find itself in a difficult position, aware of the needs of both ends of the spectrum. One way of looking at this is to say that the spiritual realm is transpersonal, the soul is both personal and transpersonal, and the material realm is personal. It's not quite as clear-cut as that, of course (what is?), but it helps us begin to get a handle on some distinctions.

The spiritual realm is owned by the All That Is Everything, the soul is owned by both the individual and the collective, and the realm of matter—that of daily life and physical survival—is owned by the individual. Why do I use the term "owned"? Because we are responsible for what we own; it is our sphere of operations, it is what we answer to. What we own also owns us. We have to look after it, clean it, fix it, carry it around, put it away after we have used it, insure it, and keep the receipt for it. Ultimately, although we may get extraordinary help and assistance regarding the material elements of life from both the spiritual realm and from the wisdom of our own souls, while we are incarnated in a physical body, the realm of matter is our responsibility to manage and organize. It's up to us to dig the garden, do the shopping, balance the checkbook, cook dinner, and make the bed.

We can't get away with not owning things because we need these things to make our lives work. Yet material stuff takes up a lot of energy. The less stuff we have, the more time we have for "non-stuff," like relationships, meditation, and dreaming. But we also need stuff because we are incarnated, and the purpose of that incarnation is to make manifest the will of heaven. For many people, it is in making the stuff of life that they find their souls. Even for a writer, who makes up intangible stories and lives in the realm of the imagination much of the time, there is nothing quite like seeing your thoughts made manifest as an actual book.

There are no easy answers here. For some people, their soul's journey might demand that they make a lot of money, build shopping malls, build bridges, and create vast edifices. For others, the work to perfect their soul might mean experiencing poverty or simplicity. The work is to discover what your soul wants and then to follow it, rather than following the herd.

## THE POWER OF THE MATERIAL REALM

Some would say that the material realm is never empty of soul. Once made, a thing exists with a kind of raw soul of existence. Once owned, it becomes imbued with the soul of its owner. It develops *numen*, power, and magic.

The things we own, the things we have made, and the things we keep around us can remind us of our soul and return us to it. If you've ever been separated from your possessions for a period of time, you know how interesting it is to be with them again. It soon becomes clear which things have real meaning for you, and what they give you energetically and emotionally.

Then there is manna, food from the gods and stuff sent directly from heaven, mentioned in the Bible. The word *mana* is the Maori word for power and magic, and is also applied to the mystery of manifestation. *Manifestation* is currently a popular word used to describe the power to generate resources, including money.

## MONEY AND THE FEMININE

The word *money* comes to us from the Latin *moneta*, meaning mint (as in money-making mint) as well as money. Moneta was also a title of the goddess Juno, in whose temple Roman money was minted. Juno Moneta was the version of Juno known as the advisor and admonisher. One of Juno's symbols was the cowrie shell, an early form of money.

Surprised? I was when I found this out. I'd always thought of money as being more male—something that men handled better than women and something they could make more easily than women could. Indeed, until the latter part of the twentieth century, marriage to a wealthy man was one of the few ways a woman could improve her material lot in life.

Juno was the wife of Jupiter, the Roman version of Zeus—the large, lustful, powerful ruler. From Jupiter we get the word *jovial*, used from ancient times as a description of those born under the influence of the planet that bore his name. Juno, as his wife, was the most important goddess in the Roman state, and was originally an ancient Italian goddess (and the name given to an asteroid discovered in 1804, interpreted by astrologers as signifying marriage on the birth chart).

In the connection between Juno and the Roman mint, we see the ancient connections laid bare between money, marriage, and the feminine. Money was originally made in the temple of the marriage goddess, the most powerful Roman depiction of the feminine. Marriage was primarily a business proposition until fairly recently: it was a contract that ensured the stability of the family and the correct raising of children. Juno was the divine representation of this marriage, and of the money that it would provide and protect. She blessed the money made in her temple with her combination of fertility and thrift.

The love that Juno represents is the love of commitment, stability, and responsibility. She is fertile without being overabundant, she is a

good manager, and she is strict and careful. Juno can be petty and
spiteful when she feels taken advantage of and threatened; she can be
generous when she feels taken care of and respected. She does not
take kindly to infidelity or disrespect, although both burden her, due
to her overexpansive, indulgent, and excessive husband.

Jupiter knows no limits, and Juno tries to reign him in, with
mixed results. Doesn't this sound like our relationship with money?
We all know people who are so careful with their money that they
never have any fun, and people who are so careless that they have lots
of fun but no stability. And most of us fluctuate in between these two
extremes, trying to manage our resources wisely but occasionally buying something we don't really need just for the heck of it.

Juno was also represented by the lily or lotus, the universal yonic
symbol. Juno conceived her son Mars without any help from her husband. Later on, the symbol of the three-lobed lily became associated
with the Virgin Mary, another goddess who conceived without a man.
(In medieval and Renaissance paintings of the Annunciation, the
moment in which Mary was infused with the Spirit, it is the archangel
Gabriel who offers her the lily).

So, here we have the awesome creative power of the spiritual
feminine—of the woman who combines her energy with that of the
Godhead. That this was seen in ancient times as the source of actual
wealth turns on its head the idea that it is men who control money
and who have easier access to it. Perhaps this is one of the missing
pieces in our current understanding of the relationship between
Spirit and matter.

## SOUL AND MONEY IN TODAY'S WORLD

We live in a time in history in which wealth has taken on a new collective meaning. There are more wealthy people than ever before, and in
the collective imagination, we have a newly created vision of a stan-
dard of living that we consider our birthright. Credit cards, mortgages,
and car loans mean we can experience ourselves as being well-off with-

out it necessarily being based in reality. Whole countries live off debt and fake money. It's all very confusing when there are still large areas of the world dealing with famine and disease on a scale that is unheard of in what is termed the "developed" world.

The inequality and illusory nature of wealth are not the only reasons to be wary of its seductions. Even if you thought you were well-off, chances are that whatever wealth you thought you possessed has diminished in recent times. The upheaval in the world's financial markets has made it only too clear that worshipping at the altar of materialism is a risky business.

So how do we navigate this treacherous territory at a time when material greed and expectation have reached heights that Socrates probably never even imagined? At a time in which global finances are in such rapid flux that no one can predict what will happen next?

First of all, stay close to yourself. Listen to your dreams and imaginings, and your inner promptings. Take yourself seriously. The soul will not lead you in the wrong direction if you pay attention. Learn to distinguish between the inner soul voice and the conditioned fantasy voice, and pay close attention to how manifestation functions for you.

The following are some questions that will help you work through your thoughts about money. Write these in your journal, and take some time to meditate on and write about each one.

- Where does your money tend to come from? Do you get funds from your family, from your spouse, from hard work, from throwing big parties, from creating works of art?

- How does money come to you? Does it come in sudden windfalls or in regular paychecks? Does it come happily or unhappily?

- What are your open gates for receiving money, and where do you think you might be closed? Visualize the gates through which money comes to you and see why some are closed. Find out what it would take to open them.

● How does stuff come to you? Is it different from how money comes to you? (Sometimes people have a knack for attracting things over money because they have a negative belief about money itself.)

● Look for where life is easy for you and see if that lesson can be applied to the realms that are more difficult. For example, if you have easy, plentiful friendships with women, think about working in a field in which women will be your clients or customers.

● Examine your family of origin issues. Every family has its trips about money. What did you learn about money as a child? If money was lacking, what concepts has that imparted to your thinking? If you were born into a family that had money and that you have inherited, accept this as your fate and use the money to further your soul dream, which will often be philanthropic and/or socially responsible.

● Look at where you disrespect money and waste it, and clean up your act. Look at your ethics and see if you feel entirely comfortable with all your choices.

● Add up how much money you spend a year in interest and see what you can do to turn that negative into a positive by earning the money before you spend it.

Gratitude practice is useful in clarifying our relationship with money. Think about all the financial help you have received in your life and give thanks for it. Gratitude blocks can often arise around money because it can be such a charged issue, bringing up issues of entitlement in particular. (Reread last month's lesson if you want to go further with the gratitude practice and money. It can completely turn around your relationship with money.)

If you feel you don't have as much money as you need, look at what useful function the lack of money might serve for you spiritually. For example, if you tend to be scattered in your thoughts and actions, a lack of money might serve to focus you on what is really necessary. Imagine having all the money you think you need and see how you feel. Within that you may find clues to why you might be blocking yourself from being wealthier.

Practice respect for but also detachment from money. The gods and goddesses of money seem to like us to pay close attention but to also be relaxed. (That applies to just about everything, though, doesn't it?)

Give space in your perceptions for the possibility that everything right now is absolutely perfect—that the restrictions you experience on the material level are actually part of the divine plan of your soul for your ultimate fulfillment. Do this while vowing to free yourself of karmic restrictions brought about by erroneous thoughts and actions regarding money, work, and material anxiety.

## SOUL AND MATTER IN HARMONY

What would it look like to have a life in which soul and matter were harmonious? Perhaps it would be no different than the way you live now, in which case, congratulations! For most of us, though, the interface between soul and matter is a continual place of work, tension, relief, joy, and conflict. This interface is the semi-permeable membrane that exists between the expansive longings of the soul and the limitations of the material dimension, and it can be both blurred and clarified by either influence.

We must follow our dreams, but only as far as the material world can stretch. If we take the dream too far, we get into trouble. If we fail to live it sufficiently, we get depressed and fall ill. We need to live at the juncture of the membrane itself, listening to both the voice of the soul and the practicalities of existence. We must have our feet firmly planted on the earth, tolerant of life's ups and downs, the changes in the seasons, and in our fates. We must do this while listening with all our heart to the inspiration from the heavens that seeks to make manifest through human creativity that vast sea of the imagination that permeates all, and is in turn fed by the steady, honest, diligent making of our souls. Just as the earth supplies our ground while we are incarnated, the soul level forms a kind of ground for the spiritual realm. Taken up to another dimension, one can imagine a realm in which a perfected soul supplies a steady ground of being for new souls coming into incarnation.

◓ ◑ ◖ ◯ ◯ ◗ ◐

May your soul know the grace that comes from acknowledging the limitations of the material realm while not being suppressed by it. May you know true abundance.

## WHAT TO DO THIS MONTH

In your journal, write about your relationship with money. Use this chapter to stimulate your inner questioning. Once you have opened up and processed your inner material, create a plan to generate greater harmony between soul and matter, and between your well-being and your material reality.

# Lesson 12
# CREATING EFFECTIVE RITUALS

● ◗ ◖ ○ ◐ ◑ ◗ ●

*Ritual sustains us as it marks the cycles of birth, growth, decay,
and renewal that sustain our lives.*
—STARHAWK, *Truth or Dare: Encounters with Power, Authority, and Mystery*

Like altars and prayer, rituals have been with human beings from the beginning of time. In fact, human life is punctuated by ritual at every turn. There are rituals for births and deaths, marriage and divorce, birthdays, celebrating special moments, going into battle, hunting animals, honoring deities, graduations, harvest and planting, fertility, and new and full moons. Almost any occasion can be the basis of a ritual.

Ritual supports and feeds the human community. It holds us together as families, clans, tribes, and nations. Increasingly in the West and all over the world, as the pace of life accelerates and people migrate, the old rituals that sustained life have fallen away. People often experience this loss of ritual and community as a spiritual emptiness in their lives. But just as we can create sacred sites in our own homes, we can create powerful and spiritually fulfilling rituals.

## WHAT IS A RITUAL?

A ritual can be a mere marker of time. It can stay at the level of ordinary consciousness, as in a birthday party, for example, or it can shift along the ritual axis into the shamanic and more purposefully spiritual realm. In this way, a ritual becomes an opportunity to shift levels of consciousness so that the divine can enter. It helps us shift our sense of reality so that we can become aware of the deeper patterning behind our lives.

We can do rituals to ask for specific kinds of help and to create specific kinds of movement in our lives. The most important element of ritual is our willingness to open up to the unknown to receive new information. This is the level and intention of ritual that I will be describing and discussing in this lesson.

## GENDER AND RITUAL

In contemporary society, in many groups and families, it is primarily women who organize and take responsibility for rituals like birthday parties, holiday gatherings, weddings, and funerals. For various reasons, women often have a strong sense of the need for the ritual marking of events and anniversaries. For one thing, women have always had the powerful occasions of menstruation, pregnancy, childbirth, and menopause to deal with. Traditionally, these momentous feminine events have been cause for ritual, and women have bonded together during these times to perform rituals together.

It's interesting to see what happens when men get involved in ritual and bring their sensibility with them. In shamanic rituals, men sometimes take the role of providing holding energy, which acts as a grounding for women's intuitive journeys.

When men and women do individual rituals, such as in a vision quest, some gender differences appear. Men sometimes need to experience more physical hardship for their ego defenses to drop away. Women often have to work through physical fear to connect with their inner knowing and spiritual guidance.

In many traditions, women and men worked separately in ritual. At Ayers Rock (Uluru) in central Australia, you can still see the men's ritual site, which is an area where the natural rock formation is shaped like an enormous phallus. Walking farther around the rock, you come to the women's ritual site, a large cave that forms a horizontal oval in the rock, shaped like a vast vulva.

Doing rituals just with one's own gender may change the energy, direction, and potential of the ritual. Some rituals feel more right to do as a group of men and boys or women and girls. Other rituals benefit enormously from having both genders involved.

## DOING RITUALS WITH OTHERS

The great thing about being an independent spiritual practitioner is that you are not dependent on an outer organization, and you can follow your own process without interference. The bad thing is that doing everything alone can feel lonely at certain stages of the journey. And sometimes we need to experience the divine with others. It can be very nourishing, fun, and affirming to do rituals with others.

While it's great to work in a group, don't let the lack of a group stop you. You only need one other person to get out of your aloneness and magnify the process. As Jesus said, "When two or more are gathered together…," and it is true that things can happen with two people that don't seem to be possible when one is alone.

When I shared a house with a friend several years ago, we did new moon and full moon rituals together for a whole year. I would draw up the astrological chart of the lunation ahead of time and have an idea of the prevailing energies, but most importantly, we opened ourselves to the energy of the moment and saw what came through. We had many illuminating experiences together as a result, and our friendship deepened. Many years ago I did a series of powerful shamanic planetary rituals with another friend that had the effect of pushing both of us along on our paths very quickly. We still talk about these rituals with a sense of awe twenty years later.

One of the by-products of having a steady independent practice is that people will inevitably ask you to help them with their spiritual needs, which often involves rituals. You may be asked to create rituals and to assist with everything—house clearings and blessings, menarche ceremonies, weddings, full moon/solstice/equinox rituals, fiftieth birthday parties, and funerals, just to name a few.

Knowing something about what works and what does not work in rituals will help you whether you are doing a ritual with people who are used to ceremony or whether you are in a more conventional setting.

## CREATING RITUALS THAT WORK

The timing of rituals is an important element in their success. A ritual is more likely to be effective if it takes place at a powerful moment, such as during a celestial event like a full or new moon, a solstice or equinox, or when there is a strong need at the time, such as for healing or for enlightenment on a troubling issue.

Intention is an equally powerful ingredient. A ritual should be empowering, not just a cozy get-together that is supportive of the known (groups of women especially can devolve into glorified coffee klatches). A ritual should take us into the greater mystery of life and bring us into contact with the sacred realms of ourselves and the unknown, unseen potential of the world.

Here are some creative ideas to consider in designing your own ritual. These ideas can work for rituals in which there is anything from one person upward, and where there is a primary goal to be open to information from Spirit during the ritual.

### THEME

First of all, consider the main theme for your ritual. It might be primarily a ritual to give thanks and to mark a blessing, such as the birth of a child, a new relationship, or a career success. It could be a commitment ritual for a marriage or major decision. Or it could be a request ritual in which you ask for help with a problem, such as money, illness, life purpose, love in general, or a specific relationship. It could also be a nature-based ritual taking place at a seasonal junction, such as a solstice or equinox or at the full or new moon.

Rituals can also combine several themes; for example, a ritual recognizing the moment of the fall equinox could also be a gratitude ritual (harvest thanksgiving) and a request ritual for information about how to orient your work during the winter months.

## PLACE

Setting up the ritual space is the first step toward tuning in to the ritual energy. First, gather artifacts that represent the main theme of the ritual. For instance, if the ritual is about love or relationship, you might use heart symbols or the color pink. You can also use pictures of gods and/or goddesses that represent love to you. You can pick roses to represent love or use special jewelry. Be creative at this stage, and let your intuition gather items for the ritual that will enhance your imaginative ability to fully enter the theme.

## COSTUME

Clothing is important for rituals. Wear something evocative that makes you feel powerful, beautiful, and inspired. Take a little time beforehand to dress, put on jewelry and makeup, and get prepared. This dressing helps you get in the mood for the ritual and already begins to alter your consciousness.

## MUSIC

Music can be a powerful way to set the mood at the beginning of a ritual. Drums are a traditional instrument often used for this purpose. If you don't have a drum, you can use a tape or CD that has music conducive to the ritual. Play it softly in background. During the bulk of the ritual, you may want to turn if off, as silence is usually preferable.

## FIRE

Fire is very useful for rituals, and being outside with a fire is very powerful. But if you can't make a fire, candles are also good. If you have a group of people, placing a small table with candles on it in the center of the group simulates the ancient experience of gathering around a fire.

## PARTICIPANTS AND ROLES

You can do rituals on your own, with a group of people or just with a friend. As mentioned earlier, the power of two or more creates synergy and maximizes the effects. Try imagining and creating a ritual with a friend. If there are more than a few of you, it's a good idea to have a designated leader who will take the group through the ritual. Otherwise, things tend to get chaotic.

## INSPIRATION

If you're stuck for inspiration as to how to design a ritual, look up ritual ideas or special prayers in books. There are many books available that provide prayers, meditations, and ideas for ritual (check the back of this book for ones I recommend). Usually you'll be able to invent a ritual yourself.

The most important thing of all is simplicity. Keep it simple. Keep it moving. It doesn't have to be long or elaborate. In fact, shorter, simple rituals can often be very effective. Have fun and be open to the spirit of the moment.

# A STEP-BY-STEP GUIDE

A ritual typically goes through several stages; having a sense of structure and form allows you to create rituals that are complete, healthy, and successful. I'm going to describe each step in detail so that you can put together your own ritual. You do not have to follow this list to the letter, but you can use it as a guide.

## STEP 1: CREATE SACRED SPACE

First you need to delineate the ritual space. If you intend to do the ritual in front of your altar, make sure the rest of the room is clean and fresh-smelling. Tidy it up, and light some incense and candles. You can also create a ritual space in any room by placing a special cloth and items on the floor, on a table, or in front of a fireplace, or by simply walking around in the shape of a circle and saying, "This is the sacred space for the ritual," or words to that effect.

If you're doing your ritual outside, a circle of trees creates a natural cathedral. Doing a ritual under a favorite tree also works well, or you can delineate a ritual space by creating a circle of stones. The edge of the ocean is a powerful place to perform a ritual as well.

You can also create the space through spoken intent. You can announce to the spirit world and to yourself that this circle is now sacred space.

Bring special items that reflect the purpose of the ritual, such as certain colors, pictures, figures, and candles. For instance, if you are doing a ritual about money, you could place within the sacred space your wallets, checkbooks, gold jewelry, and other objects that reflect abundance or prosperity.

## STEP 2: PURIFY THE SPACE

Now that you have delineated the space, it's time to purify it and the participants. One way to do this is by smudging the space and everyone present with sage. As described in Lesson 1, sage is a common herb used by Native Americans to purify the atmosphere. Simply walk around the space and blow the smoke around the environment as you go. Let the sacred cleansing smoke brush over each participant's back and front. It is important to be silent during the purification phase, and to focus on the sense of clarity and calm created by the purification phase. You can also use incense for the same purpose. Add lavender to the sage to bring in beauty, cedar to bring in the energy of the wise grandparent spirits, and copal (tree resin used in Central America) to open the third eye and enhance visioning.

Drumming is another traditional way to cleanse the environment. As a drum is struck, its sound waves travel through the air, dispelling and breaking up any stagnant or negative energy. Drumming also helps us come into our bodies and feel connected to the earth as we allow the drum to vibrate through our being.

Singing is another traditional way to purify the atmosphere. It's similar to beating the drum, except the vibrational sounds are created within our own bodies. You can use different songs to create different atmospheres, depending on the occasion.

Purifying the space bonds the participants in sacred time and space, and mentally and physically prepares them for the journey ahead.

(For more detailed information on space clearing, see Lesson 1, "Creating Sacred Space.")

## STEP 3: ATTUNE AND GROUND THE ENERGY

This is the moment when you all focus together for the ritual. (If you are working by yourself, modify this for one person.) You can do this by singing, holding hands, or making a connection to the earth through a simple grounding exercise that involves deep breathing or feeling the energy of the earth moving up through your feet.

This part of the ritual is also where you acknowledge and pay respects to the local spirits of the land, unseen forces, and spirit guardians. It can be a short statement that pays homage to whatever forces or spirits may be present. These entities can include nature spirits, angels, personal spirit guides, and religious figures. Simply acknowledge them, and thank them for being present.

## STEP 4: PRAY FOR PROTECTION AND GUIDANCE

Asking for protection and guidance is important to do at the beginning of a ritual because it brings in the spirit guides in a respectful way. It tells the participants' unconscious that it is safe to shift levels of consciousness. You make a simple request that you be protected and guided safely through the ritual.

Also, ask that the information you receive be of the highest integrity and that the spirits drawn to your sacred space are only there to wish you well. Just as when you have a party you invite people you like and trust, so it is with inviting spirits into your ritual.

During this stage, we begin to enter what native Australians call the dreamtime and what Carlos Castaneda called the *nagual:* when the veil between the worlds begins to lift. Feeling this energy shift can be a little scary, especially in the beginning, and knowing that you have protection and the right kind of guidance calms any fears.

## STEP 5: STATE YOUR INTENT

This is where you say why you are doing the ritual. If you are doing the ritual alone, state the purpose of the ritual. If you are doing a ritual as a group, say why you are gathering together. For instance, you might say that you are gathered together tonight under the full moon to celebrate your creativity and fullness as women. Or you might say that you are gathered together under the new moon to receive information about creating money in your life. Or you might have come together primarily to pray together to send healing energy to people in distress in a particular part of the world. Or to ask for healing for yourselves as a group, or one member in particular. One of you might be facing a big decision and want help finding clarity on a specific issue. Whatever the purpose of your ritual, now is the time to make the intention explicit.

## STEP 6: EXPLORE THE FOUR INNER STAGES

The next four stages form the bulk, or the substance, of the ritual. The following stages are suggestions, and you can fill these stages with whatever activities you feel moved to do. They could include making things, singing, dancing, visualizations, silent prayer, movement, offerings, and meditation, as well as the ideas presented here.

The first stage is **Invocation**. What specific energies or deities (internal or external) do you want present? Who and what do you need for this ritual to happen? For instance, if you are doing a ritual to ask for guidance in matters of love and sexuality, you might ask Aphrodite, the Greek goddess of love, to be present. If you are doing a ritual around forgiveness, you might ask Quan Yin, the Chinese goddess of compassion, to be present. You can ask an ancestor to be present, such as a favorite grandparent or someone famous in history. You can ask for a nature spirit such as the spirit of fire or water, or an angel or spiritual teacher. You can even ask for the energy of one of the astrological signs, such as the majestic, fertile energy of Taurus, the bull. If you're not sure whom to invite, you can simply ask that the appropriate person or being come to you to help with the ritual. Then wait quietly with your eyes closed and see what being or beings appear before your eyes.

When you ask sincerely, a being will always come. Believe in your perceptions and do not doubt them. You may see something or hear a name in your mind. You may get a multisensory impression, as in a dream. When a god/goddess or being appears before you, ask them why he or she has come to you and listen to the response. These archetypal beings exist in the collective mind, and we can connect with them when we approach the process with humility and respect.

The second stage is **Release/Letting Go**. This stage is about letting go of whatever thoughts, beliefs, moods, or obstacles appear to be impeding you in life. To start this stage, simply feel whatever it is inside of you that feels resistant to the flow of your life, or feels blocked and stuck. As you identify and feel the resistance, feel its energy dynamic leaving your field.

The third stage is **Receiving/Desires**. In this stage, you ask for what you want and then open up to that which you desire. For instance, if it's more love you want in your life, feel the energy of love coming into your space. If it's more money or more sense of purpose, feel those energies coming into your space. This is also the part of the ritual where you receive guidance and instruction on how to achieve your goals, live your life, or heal yourself. Listen for the information by opening up your inner ears and inner mind, and then let the information come to you, however it wants to. Perhaps you will hear a voice, see images, feel emotions, experience strong body sensations, hear sounds, or feel like moving in specific ways.

The fourth stage is **Gratitude**. This last stage is where you give thanks for all the many blessings in your life, for the ritual itself, and for whatever information, guidance, or healing you received. This is also a time to be silent, and simply let Spirit speak to you and give you any final information.

## STEP 7: CLOSE THE CIRCLE AND DEDICATE THE MERIT

It's important to give a ritual a definitive close when you end it. Otherwise all your hard work and energy tends to just disperse unproductively. Don't go unconscious at the end of a ritual and let things disintegrate. Close the ritual as consciously as you began it.

This part of the ritual allows the participants to return to normal space and time and the everyday world. You can close a ritual by holding hands, drumming, singing, clapping, or simply making a statement of closure such as, "We now end the ritual and close this sacred space."

Dedication of the merit is a Buddhist tradition that can be incorporated into any ritual and is a crucial part of closing the ritual. You offer up the energy or merit of the ritual by dedicating it to those who need healing or assistance at this time. It's a way of spreading the goodwill and energy around, and it also helps get us to go beyond our own egos by offering our energy and love to others. You simply say, "We dedicate the merit of this ritual to _____." You can dedicate the merit to all sentient beings, or you can be more specific. Participants can add names of people they want to send healing energy to or say something general, like all people on the planet living in war zones or battered women. Be open to the moment. Some prayer that you had not planned at all may come in at this point, and it is able to come through you because you have been opened up to greater spiritual awareness by the ritual.

## STEP 8: END / WALK AWAY

Finally, pack any items you used, disassemble the space, and walk away. Don't hang around in the same space if you can help it. Make a physical demarcation by going to another room or outdoors. If you are going to eat together and celebrate, do it in another room. If you have to use the same room, make sure everyone goes out and comes back in, and that you smudge the room in between.

Now let go of the ritual, and return to your everyday space and time.

———— ∞∞∞ ————

## WHAT TO DO THIS MONTH

This month, do a ritual, either alone or with others. Make
notes in your journal afterwards about what you experienced,
and watch your dreams for further input, especially the night
after the ritual.

# Lesson 13

# INTEGRATION, INTENTION, AND ACTIVATION

◐ ● ◑ ○ ○ ◑ ● ◐

The natural state of the soul is freedom.
We will know we are free the moment we surrender totally
to the perfection of life in each moment.
—RESHAD FEILD, *The Last Barrier: A Journey into the Essence of Sufi Teachings*

So here we are, at the last of our thirteen lessons. It's been a challenge and a joy to gather together and put into words the many and varying threads of spiritual knowledge that I have picked up over the last thirty years—longer than that if you include my religious childhood and early metaphysical inclinations. As so often happens, I've been finding out more about the subject as I've been writing, drawing on things I had forgotten, and integrating what I know and have experienced into a digestible form through the act of writing about it. Action is one of the keys to integration. You just have to do it, even if you don't really know why.

For example, meditation doesn't feel that good for a lot of people to start with. It can take awhile for the benefits to make themselves apparent. Often the only reason to begin is the example of other people who do it. It's the same with writing down one's dreams. It seems like so much gobbledygook to begin with. Why bother? But if you do, the dreaming stream gets clearer, and you learn about your own mind and soul. To develop spiritually, we have to take actions to accompany and actualize our good intentions.

159

When I was writing these lessons, I had a series of spiritual dreams. As I was finishing up the lessons, I dreamed about the core issues involved in integration.

In the first dream, I was looking at an old wall. As I stared at it, writing became revealed, as if it were written in invisible ink that was now showing itself. The writing was in the ancient languages—Sanskrit, Latin, and Arabic—a line of each. I knew each line of writing said the same thing in different languages, but I couldn't understand what the writing said. Then at the bottom of the wall the words emerged in English. It said, "There is nothing wrong with you." Then God showed up as a crazy man wearing rags and surrounded by a bunch of people dancing wildly, some spastically, and all very happy, and all knowing there was nothing wrong with them or with anything. They grabbed my hands and pulled me into this silly, goofy, utterly unself-conscious dance.

In the second dream, I was talking to someone who was a Christian but had difficulty relating to God. I told her it's easier if you understand that there isn't just one God, and I showed her how there was a god for everyone, hovering above their heads and attached by an etheric umbilical cord to the crown chakra. In this dream, the higher self and God were the same thing. "Oh," she said, "there are as many gods as there are people!"

This dream cracked something open in me—a frozen place I hadn't known I had. Although I thought intellectually that I could talk to God, that one could have a direct line to the divine, I was still partly stuck in the idea that I wasn't worthy of that. After the dream, I was able to connect my daily experience of being fed wisdom and information with a direct experience of God, without the sense that this was a kind of hubris. Without really being aware that this was what I thought, I had been laboring under a clouded notion that the higher self, simply because it was connected to me, was inherently not quite God, not as good as God; God was something unreachable, sublime, and separate. Maybe my higher self could talk to God, but my higher self wasn't God. Of course, that's the inheritance from my religious background, and it is a pervasive concept in the culture. After this dream, that perception changed, and I began to feel that there really was no distinction to be made between my higher self and God. It was the final end of the God-is-an-old-man-with-a-beard-in-the-sky notion.

The two dreams go together, in that you have to get that there is nothing inherently wrong with accepting that God is connected to you. And for the latter to make any kind of sense, you have to completely drop the idea of one God in an anthropomorphic sense. Yes, metaphysically one can say that all those gods are more alike than they are not, and that in some sense there is one God just as there is one human, with the same basic structure that we all share. But the variations within that are manifold.

So we have the relationship with our personal God—our higher self. Keeping this connection open is really why we meditate, write down our dreams, pay attention to background thoughts, read spiritual texts, and try to keep ourselves energetically clear. We are connecting in this way with our inner truth, and that inner truth is also a spiritual truth—God's truth, if you like. Some of that truth will be somewhat universal (practicing loving kindness, for example) and some of it is specific and personal. None of it should ever be assumed to be another person's inner truth. If we all have our own God, we can once and for all let go of the notion that we have any kind of spiritual superiority as a result of whatever spiritual path or religion we practice.

This personal sense of God/Spirit streams outward and connects us into universal consciousness: our collective, ancient understanding and sensibility of the power and meaning of existence. There is universal agreement across all religions and peoples about what we can call the Source, the collective and originating core spirit of life. The universal agreement is that this source is love.

## INTEGRATION

Whenever we go through any strong experience and whenever we learn something new, we always have to integrate the experience for the new information to have lasting value (rather than just confusing us and being quickly forgotten). Sometimes this happens without any effort, but we often need to apply our consciousness to the process. If we don't make a conscious effort to integrate spiritual practice and experience within our whole consciousness, it can remain somehow distant from the rest of life and lose its effect as a result.

Integration shows itself through your state of mind and through how you navigate the world. Your overall level of integration shows itself most radically in how you handle the extremes of stress/excitement and boredom/sameness. When we go through a lot of change, we tend to fragment a little mentally until we have integrated the new material. There is so much change today that many people get stressed out easily, and they are also quickly bored.

When you integrate your prior experience and your current reality at a deep level, you have full access to yourself and can live from a genuine wholeness. You are attractive to others, your energy shines, and there is a certain glow about you.

In terms of actualizing one's potential, full integration is both the hardest and the easiest part of the spiritual journey: it is the hardest because it is the crucial step that will change everything forever; it is the easiest because if you have done the work (which can mean all sorts of things—forty years of meditation, thirty lifetimes, simply showing up for your life on a daily basis, or an inexplicable act of grace), at a certain point, integration just happens.

This is for sure the hardest step to analyze and describe. How does our spiritual self become fully actualized through our physical and emotional bodies? Can we prevent it? Can we stall the process? Is it fated? Can we speed it up?

Along the way, we integrate incrementally. You will know when you need to integrate an experience or a piece of information because you will feel out of sorts, stuck, without energy, and depressed. You may go back into an old addictive pattern and beat yourself up mentally. At these times, something is trying to fit itself together, and until it does, you will find yourself tired or disturbed and uneasy, even if just a little.

The trouble is that when we feel disturbed is when we most need to practice. And it's just when we least feel like doing the work. Even though we may have tools at our disposal, sometimes we just can't sit on the cushion to recite a mantra, read a spiritual text, write down our dreams, or think clearly about anything at all.

At those times the work does still go on despite our resistance, and it takes place in some subterranean, hidden part of the self. There is a deep mystery to the path of the psyche toward wholeness, in the relationship of the soul to Spirit. But despite this mystery, there are some tricks for bypassing the grumpy and stubborn aspect of the psyche—to make things easier on ourselves and to haul us out of the misery of resistance.

These are the main methods to help integration:

## REGULAR PRACTICE

Sometimes life deals us a hard blow and our spiritual resilience is tested. We all have periods of turning away from our spiritual self, our beliefs, and our knowledge that there is more to life than the material realm. At times we lose our balance and may, even for a moment, experience a sense of bitterness and of victimization.

Everyone has bad days. Some of us have bad months and years. This is where regular practice can really help you. For example, there was a time when I had a bad week—not a major trauma, just a particularly bad week—in which I had a professional setback, a relationship went sour, and I got the flu. I felt terrible. I stopped meditating for three days. What was the point? I didn't care. I felt worse and worse. Then on the fourth day, I found myself setting out the cushion, lighting the candles, and sitting down, without having planned it or coerced myself into it. It's a habit, and like any habit, sometimes I do it without thinking about it first.

The art of living lies in cultivating good habits because it is one's habits that show most strongly in hard times. That brief meditation helped set me back on track. I began writing again, I paid attention to my dreams, and life came back into perspective. It wasn't a magic bullet: I still didn't feel great. There were things that tugged at me, and I still felt a bit heavy in my soul. But I was moving toward wellness in myself and not stagnating in the pit of self-pity.

The one element that is shared by all the religions is the belief that regular practice of prayer or meditation, or some kind of devotional and centering behavior, is helpful on the spiritual path. Cultivating such a habit is one surefire way to keep up with your life, and to continually integrate your life experiences, your inner state, and your spiritual guidance.

## EMOTION

Unacknowledged and unfelt emotion clogs our energy being and prevents full integration of experience. Many people suffer from an inability to be emotionally present due to various factors. It could be that an event was too complex or powerful to process all the emotions that arose at the time, or that you were trained as a child not to express emotion clearly and straightforwardly. Cultures and families vary in this regard. It's one thing to learn to control your feelings in public situations, which is an important aspect of growing up, but it's another if you suppress those feelings with yourself and those you are closest to. If you were raised in a family or culture that taught you to repress your feelings all the time, you will need to learn how to be in a fuller relationship with your feeling life; otherwise much of your life will remain unintegrated.

Journal writing, talking with a good friend, and counseling/ therapy are all very good ways to connect with your feelings. By exploring and expressing feelings in these ways, they are acknowledged and released, and we learn from their wisdom.

## RELATIONSHIP

We also find keys to integration through our relationships with other beings—with our lovers, partners, children, parents, siblings, friends, colleagues, and pets. Soul sharing can occur in many ways, and it is one of the primary ways we build on and support our growing spiritual wholeness.

Any of these relationships can foster your spiritual development, but it is often through friendship that this happens most harmoniously because there tends to be less compulsion and projection in friendship, and more space and freedom. To Aristotle, friendship was "one soul inhabiting two bodies."[6]

We can also integrate a lot of material through sexuality, which is one of the reasons people miss sex when they don't have it, and why people who lead very intense lives in the public eye often have crazy sex lives. It's a subconscious attempt to integrate by connecting with the instinctual core. Sex can be tremendously healing and realigning after a difficult or demanding experience, and it can be all the more so when lovemaking is accompanied by consciousness and full emotional participation.

Pets can be of tremendous help in aiding integration. Their very presence is calming, and their regular needs keep you grounded. Dogs and horses need exercise, so they make you get out of the house and into the fresh air. Walking with a dog is a really good way to gently come to center and integrate the day's events. And if you don't have a dog, just walk anyway! Fresh air and the rhythm of steady walking, especially out in nature, are great aids to integration.

## SONG AND DANCE

Integration happens naturally through movement and action. It doesn't seem to happen just by thinking about things or wishing for them. One of the quickest ways to integrate an experience is to make up a song and dance to represent it.

In the ancient healing center at Epidaurus in Greece, people created drama together as part of their healing regime. Through making plays about their experiences, they found deep psychological healing that then translated to the physical body.

---

6. Aristotle quoted in *Lives and Opinions of Eminent Philosophers*, by Diogenes Laertius, third century.

We can also see this link among dance, song, and integration in ritual and magic, where there is often an accompanying song and dance to go with a prayer or intention. Dance is the big missing piece in most contemporary religious practice. The songs are still there, but there is rarely any accompanying dancing.

If you want to quickly process anything, make up a song and a dance about it. Spontaneously. It's surprisingly easy to do. (This is another key element in manifestation, by the way.)

## CREATIVITY

We also foster and experience integration through creative acts such as writing, painting, gardening, and cooking. Doing a collage is a wonderful way of integrating a phase of your life or a particular experience. Pick a theme and create a collage with the theme in mind. Or just do a random collage, letting your unconscious choose pictures simply because you are drawn to them. This is like having a waking dream. Once the collage is done, you will be able to see a theme or an echoing motif.

I love to cook after I've been through something powerful. I head for the kitchen, and find the integration and inner settling I need by stirring a pot of soup, mixing a cake, or kneading bread dough. On a daily basis, just to stay current and properly absorb the day's events, cooking can be a wonderful balance to a busy life. People often think they're too tired to cook, but the act of cooking itself is one of the best de-stressers we have.

A big chunk of tiredness is actually unprocessed feeling and experience. If you cook, write in your journal, or dance around your house, you'll find your energy comes pouring back in. That's because you have integrated and processed the day through these actions: through moving your body, through making something, and through creativity.

Life is alchemy, after all, so any alchemical act such as cooking, deep sexuality, gardening, or throwing a pot—anything in which one thing gives birth to something else and a transformation takes place—

helps us integrate. Creativity keeps us in the flow of life, helping us integrate what has happened and move forward into the next phase.

## INTENTION

Setting goals and new intentions is ritualized into our annual rhythm. On New Year's Day, more people set goals than at any other time of the year. If New Year's Day doesn't resonate for you, then your birthday is as good or even better for setting goals. It's your new sun cycle—your personal New Year. What is good about the New Year that begins on January 1 is that it is shared. It's a collective new beginning, and that can help because, when we do something en masse, it can acquire extra strength and impetus.

It's a good idea to do some integration of the last year before you set your intentions for the coming one. Write down the salient moments, achievements, trials, successes, joys, realizations, and decisions from the past year. Then, sitting firmly in the present moment, you can move naturally into seeing the year ahead of you and feel into your intention for the coming time.

Ask yourself, what are my deepest intentions for this year? Take some time to think about these intentions, to intuit the coming year, and to sense what you need at this time in your life. Then write down your intentions.

Intentions demand action, but just one step at a time. Actions always lead somewhere and move things along. So when you make your New Year resolutions, think about and write down what actions you are going to take to make your goals a reality.

Do you want to be in a relationship? Tell your friends you are looking for someone. One woman I know had business cards printed up with her requirements for a mate on them, and she handed them out to everyone she met. She did meet a man through this rather extreme and very gutsy method, and they are still happily together ten years later. If that feels like a bit much for you, then at least you can sign up with an online dating site. You may not meet anyone there, but you will have to articulate who you are and what you want. It gets you into the energy stream of partnership.

Do you want to strengthen your meditation practice? Make a plan for accommodating more meditation time into your daily schedule.

Do you want to make more money? Make a business/finance plan for next year, and make sure it is a realistic plan for how to attract the money you need. Then do an action that will move you nearer to that outcome. It's a good idea to do an accompanying action every day and at the same time of day, if you can.

## ACTIVATION

Activation occurs every time we set an intention and make an accompanying action. The more frequently and resolutely you activate your energy field with intention and action, the easier it will be for you to live a life of satisfying service both to others and to your own higher self. And through doing this, the more integrated and therefore whole you will become.

This willingness to activate the fruit of one's practice should be happening all the time, not waiting for a bolt of enlightenment or a sense of perfection. You can activate your spirit and offer something to the world around you every day.

## SUMMARY

Integration can't be rushed. Integration comes from a routine of good daily habits that encourage listening to your inner voice / higher self, such as meditation, writing down your dreams, keeping a journal, and allowing some open time in the midst of your day to process and stay up to date with yourself.

We integrate through action, whether that be through a spiritual practice like meditation; relationships and talking things through; expression such as song, dance, and writing in a journal; physical activity; or making things with our hands. Allowing ourselves to feel and to acknowledge our feelings also aids in integration and knits us into a fuller connectivity with our whole selves in current time. We integrate through sleeping, dreaming, relaxing and playing, so make enough time for these.

Integration is fed by our intention, which sets our forward movement. Intention clarifies our energy field. And activation of our deepest self arises naturally when we combine intention with conscious action.

Then there is the integration of who we are with the desire to serve, which naturally leads us to give of ourselves to the world. The Dalai Lama often cites the following stanza as his greatest source of inspiration:

> *For as long as space remains,*
> *For as long as sentient beings remain,*
> *Until then, may I too remain*
> *And dispel the miseries of the world.*

Nothing really counts until we give it back. We don't know fully that we have integrated anything until the urge to share it comes over us and we give freely of ourselves, fully entering the stream of life.

# ACKNOWLEDGMENTS

Fight First of all, deep and abiding thanks to my mother and father, Jennifer and Derek Owen, who took me to church and sent me to Sunday School, thoughtfully discussed metaphysical and moral matters with me as I was growing up, and still nourish me with their wisdom, love, and support.

Thank you to all my spiritual sisters and brothers: friends of the path who have entered sacred space with me to mutually celebrate, commiserate, thank, share, release, love, bless, teach, learn, and inspire.

Two longstanding and treasured friends, both wise, deep, and gentle women, deserve special mention: Victoria Cresswell, for being such a steadfast ally, for her nurturing spirit and healing skills so generously shared, and for all our ceremonies and spiritual adventures; and Gemma Summers, for bringing her crystal-clear focus, warm heart, ability to synthesize, and sense of fun to our co-created rituals and co-taught workshops; for ongoing conversations at the interface of psychology and spirituality, and for her contribution to the chapters on altars and rituals.

Deep gratitude to Jeff Littlefield and David Brown for leading me into the wild, and for sharing inspiring travels to sacred places.

I thank and bless the spirits of Andrew Murray, Kevin Wreford, and Balthazar Bear, three sensitive and beautiful beings (two human and one canine) who accompanied me with love and caring at different stages of the journey, and who all passed over, each of them suddenly, in the past year.

Thank you to the spiritual teachers in whose presence I have sat and with whom I have studied, too many to name all, but I would especially like to thank His Holiness the Dalai Lama and Lama Tsultrim Allione. Joan Halifax, and Gay Luce and her mystery school significantly informed my understanding of how spiritual practice is enhanced by the relationship with the natural world and the translation of traditional practices into contemporary ritual.

Thank you to all the healers, psychotherapists, and counselors who helped me integrate spiritual experience with psychological understanding and physical well-being. Thanks especially to Arnold Mindell and everyone I trained with at the Process Work Institutes in Zürich and Portland, and to Sophia Sharpe, Jane Easty, and Jan Mojsa. Special thanks to Susan Jeter for her warm friendship; conversations about healing, embodiment, and spirituality; and for being so tuned in wherever on the planet I might wander to.

I wrote this book while sequestered in a midlife retreat in a village in southwest France, living in the shadow of a huge and ancient abbey, and walking on cobbled streets that had been trodden upon by pilgrims from all over Europe since the eighth century. It was a blessed interlude away from the stresses and stimulations of modern life, living in a world in which everything stopped for three hours at lunchtime, and my neighbor prayed to the Virgin Mary for me on the rare occasions when I had to go away. Most of the time, I lived very simply without a car and alone with my dog, the aforementioned splendid Balthazar. I give thanks for the magic of that place, for the friendship and generosity of its inhabitants, and for the gift of those years in which time felt abundant and my mind found a deeper calm, out of which this book emerged. Many people there helped me in various ways. In particular I thank Roger and Tsila Hurst, Nese and Remy Pelt, Suzanne l'Hoste, Robin Dillon-Mahon, Stefan Volland and Britta Jacob, Vicky Wisher, Ann Mason and Peter Welsford, Angela Thymides and Hans Valkhoff, Maria Pietri and Fernand, Rose Fabre, Mme. Lauta, Susannah Bluestein-Grover and Paul Grover. Many thanks also to Adrienne Momi for the gift of an inspiring journey to Florence and Siena.

During the previous fifteen years, I had lived on the West Coast of the United States, where I had many spiritual adventures; met many teachers; and was helped, homed, and loved by many people. I give great thanks to everyone who assisted me so openheartedly and especially to Raymond Himmel, Michael Waterhouse, Deborah Fallender, David Brown and family, Jackie Redner and Scott Shapiro, Noelle and Arthur Imparato, Annie Azzaritti, Noah Morowitz, Nalini Chilkov, Susan Kirk, Kathleen Pouls, Kit Berskovich and Ken Weisner, Ted Behlendorf, and, last but not least, Kip Wood, for being a true spiritual friend and accomplice in exploring different practices and faiths.

Many thanks to David Garbacz for making the vital publishing connection, to Cynthia Black and the team at Beyond Words, and to Anne Lawrance, Gill Bailey, Zoë Goodkin and everyone involved with the publication of this edition at Piatkus and the Little, Brown Book Group. Many thanks to Elizabeth Haylett Clark at the Society of Authors for contract advice.

Lastly, I give my deep thanks to all the people who have studied and worked with me over the past thirty years, whose attention to the work, willingness to explore, and openness to their individual journeys have been a constant inspiration.

# SUGGESTIONS FOR
# FURTHER READING

● ◑ ◐ ○ ○ ◐ ◑ ●

**Introduction: The Independent Path**

Andrew Harvey, *The Direct Path: Creating a Personal Journey to the Divine Using the World's Spiritual Traditions* (New York: Broadway, 2000).

Joel Kramer and Diana Alstad, *The Guru Papers: Masks of Authoritarian Power* (Berkeley, CA: Frog, Ltd., 1993).

**Lesson 1: Creating Sacred Space**

Laura Cerwinske, *In a Spiritual Style: The Home as Sanctuary* (New York: Thames and Hudson, 1998).

Denise Linn, *Space Clearing: How to Purify and Create Harmony in Your Home* (London: Ebury, 2000).

**Lesson 2: Making Altars**

Sandra Kynes, *Your Altar: Creating a Sacred Space for Prayer and Meditation* (Woodbury, MN: Llewellyn, 2007).

**Lesson 3: Personal History and Motivation**

There are many inspiring biographies and autobiographies of people who have led spiritually focused lives of great transformation and service. Reading these books can be enormously helpful to those pursuing a path of independent spiritual practice. Here are some suggestions:

Tsultrim Allione, *Women of Wisdom* (Ithaca, NY: Snow Lion, 2000).

Peter Caddy, *In Perfect Timing* (Findhorn: Findhorn Press, 1995).

Reshad Feild, *The Last Barrier: A Journey into the Essence of Sufi Teachings* (Herndon, VA: Lindisfarne, 2002).

Jim Forest, *Living with Wisdom: A Life of Thomas Merton* (New York: Orbis Books, 1991).

China Galland, *Longing for Darkness: Tara and the Black Madonna* (New York: Penguin, 2007).

Vicky Mackenzie, *Cave in the Snow: Tenzin Palmo's Quest for Enlightenment* (New York: Bloomsbury, 1998).

**Lesson 4: Clearing the Mind and Grounding the Body**

William Bloom, *The Endorphin Effect: A Breakthrough Strategy for Holistic Health and Spiritual Wellbeing* (London: Piatkus, 2001).

Arnold Mindell, *Working on Yourself Alone: Inner Dreambody Work* (Portland, OR: Lao Tse Press, 2001).

———, *Working with the Dreaming Body* (Portland, OR: Lao Tse Press, 2001).

**Lesson 5: Meditation, Prayer, and Spiritual Guidance**

Elizabeth Roberts and Elias Amidon, *Earth Prayers from Around the World: 365 Prayers, Poems, and Invocations for Honoring the Earth* (New York: HarperSanFrancisco, 1991).

Jack Kornfield, *Meditation for Beginners* (Louisville, CO: Sounds True, 2008).

Don Miguel Ruiz, *Prayers: A Communion with Our Creator* (San Rafael, CA: Amber-Allen, 2001).

Maggie Oman Shannon, *The Way We Pray: Celebrating Spirit from Around the World* (Berkeley, CA: Conari, 2001).

## Lesson 6: Dreams and Developing the Imagination

Robert Bosnak, *A Little Course in Dreams* (Boston: Shambhala, 1998).

C. G. Jung, *Memories, Dreams, Reflections* (New York: Vintage, 1989).

Connie Kaplan, *Dreams Are Letters from the Soul: Discover the Connections Between Your Dreams and Your Spiritual Life* (New York: Harmony Books, 2002).

Jill Mellick, *The Art of Dreaming: Tools for Creative Dream Work* (Berkeley, CA: Conari 2001).

## Lesson 7: Divination and Developing the Intuition

Ann Fiery, *The Book of Divination* (San Francisco: Chronicle Books, 1999).

Paul D. O'Brien, *Divination: Sacred Tools for Reading the Mind of God* (Portland, OR: Visionary Networks Press, 2007).

## Lesson 8: Spiritual Practice and the Natural World

Judith Boice, *Mother Earth* (San Francisco: Sierra Club Books, 1992).

Robert Macfarlane, *The Wild Places* (London: Granta, 2007).

John O'Donohue, *Anam Cara: A Book of Celtic Wisdom* (New York: HarperCollins, 1998).

Jim PathFinder Ewing, *Finding Sanctuary in Nature: Simple Ceremonies in the Native American Tradition for Healing Yourself and Others* (Findhorn: Findhorn Press, 2007).

## Lesson 9: Sacred Time Alone: Vision Quest and Retreat

Steven Bailey, *The Fasting Diet* (New York: McGraw-Hill, 2001).

Steven Foster, *Book of Vision Quest* (New York: Fireside, 1989).

Lara Owen, *Her Blood Is Gold: Awakening to the Wisdom of Menstruation* (Wimborne, UK: Archive Publishing, 2008).

**Lesson 10: Gratitude, Wonder, and Acceptance**

Sarah Ban Breathnach, *Simple Abundance Journal of Gratitude* (New York: Grand Central Publishing, 1996).

M. J. Ryan, *Attitudes of Gratitude: How to Give and Receive Joy Every Day of Your Life* (Berkeley, CA: Conari, 1999).

P. L. Travers, *Mary Poppins* (London: Harper Collins Children's Books 2008).

**Lesson 11: Spiritual Practice and the Material Realm**

Walter Lubeck, *The Tao of Money* (Twin Lakes, WI: Lotus Press, 2000).

Alan Seale, *The Manifestation Wheel: A Practical Process for Creating Miracles* (San Francisco: Red Wheel Weiser, 2008).

**Lesson 12: Creating Effective Rituals**

Steven Farmer, *Sacred Ceremony: How to Create Ceremonies for Healing, Transitions, and Celebrations* (London: Hay House, 2004).

John O'Donohue, *To Bless the Space Between Us: A Collection of Invocations and Blessings* (audiobook) (Louisville, CO: Sounds True, 2008).

**Lesson 13: Integration, Intention, and Activation**

Tsultrim Allione, *Feeding Your Demons: Ancient Wisdom for Resolving Inner Conflict* ( London: Hay House, 2009).

Don Miguel Ruiz, *The Four Agreements: A Practical Guide to Personal Freedom* (San Rafael, CA: Amber-Allen, 1997).

# RESOURCES

● ◐ ○ ○ ○ ◐ ● ◐

**Caduceus:** A spirituality magazine founded in the UK in 1987, focusing on psychological, emotional, spiritual, ecological and environmental health, therapy and growth. Good resource for information at the interface of spirituality, environmentalism and healthcare.
*caduceus.info*

**Foundation for Holistic Spirituality:** An organization based in the United Kingdom for networking, representing, and supporting holistic spirituality.
*f4hs.org*
PO Box 3660, Glastonbury BA6 8ZY, United Kingdom
Telephone: +44 (0) 7940 001394

**Sacred Hoop Magazine:** A magazine founded in the UK in 1993, focused on ancient sacred traditions, sacred living, and global wisdom. Great place to look for ads on workshops and retreats.
*sacredhoop.org*

## SUPPLIES

**Blue Banyan:** Wide range of ethically produced products for meditation, yoga, and bodywork.
*bluebanyan.co.uk*

**Devotion:** online store based in London, with lovely selection of items for altars and sacred adornment.
*devotion.co.uk*

**Pink Lotus:** Buddhist-oriented suppliers of meditation and altar items with excellent service and reasonable prices.
*pinklotus.co.uk*

**Sounds True:** Great source for audio CDs by a wide range of contemporary spiritual teachers.
*shop.soundstrue.com*

## RETREAT CENTERS

**Esalen Institute:** The original retreat center for the human potential movement, founded in 1962 in an unbeatable location overlooking the Pacific at Big Sur, CA with hot springs. Offers a wide range of retreats on alternative education and personal transformation.
*esalen.org*

**Gaia House:** a retreat centre in Devon established in the 1930s, offers retreats from various Buddhist traditions led by teachers from all over the world, for first-timers as well those wishing to broaden or deepen an established meditation practice.
*gaiahouse.co.uk*

**Holy Island**, off the West Coast of Scotland: this ancient place of worship today is home to the *Centre for World Peace and Health*

which offers retreats and courses by an eclectic range of teachers for mind, body and spirit.
*holyisland.org*

**Omega:** Founded in 1977 and situated in Rhinebeck, NY with branches in Manhattan and Boston. Omega offers day, weekend, and weeklong workshops on personal growth as well as professional trainings in yoga, psychology, and leadership. Rest and rejuvenation retreats also available.
*eomega.org*

**Spirit Rock Meditation Center:** A retreat center in Marin County established in the mid-1980s, focusing on insight meditation (Vipassana).
*spiritrock.org*

**The Soulful Woman:** retreats for women in Australia and Bali designed to replenish body, mind and spirit, to create a greater balance in the cycle of giving and receiving, and to explore and nourish women's sacred inner life and self-care.
*www.facebook.com/thesoulfulwoman*

**Tara Mandala Retreat Center:** Located in the peaceful, inspiring mountains of southwest Colorado. Offers a wide range of retreats (chiefly Tibetan Buddhism but also natural medicine, yoga, and psychology) and beautiful cabins for individual retreats.
*taramandala.org*

## FURTHER STUDY

**Chalice Centre and Avalon Mystery School:** Tuition in Celtic spirituality and the British Mystery tradition online, and tours to sacred sites.
*chalicecentre.net* and *avalonmysteryschool.net*

**The Foundation for Shamanic Studies:** Training programs in shamanism and shamanic healing.
*shamanism.org*

**Lara Owen:** Individual consultations, talks, and workshops on spirituality and personal development in the US and UK.
*laraowen.com*

**Planetary Energies:** Lara Owen's blog exploring the connections between the planets, the cycle of the seasons, the ancient holy days, and today's world.
*planetaryenergies.net*

**Turtle Dreamers:** Online dreamspace for teaching, encouraging and sharing dream awareness and understanding.
*turtledreamers.com*